MIND YOUR OWN BUSIN€SS

Also by Feargal Quinn

CROWNING THE CUSTOMER
How to Become Customer-Driven

Praise for this international business best-seller:

'Customer service is simple, focused and about engaging your
people first. Feargal's book shows you how to do this.'
Allen Leighton, Chairman, Royal Mail

'No theory is advanced without practical, entirely convincing,
examples. And not a single instance of management-speak. The very
best businessmen will be the first to welcome this splendid book.'
Sir Martin Sorrell, CEO, WPP

'Many say the customer is king or queen, but seldom mean it. For
Feargal it is the truth. He cares about everyone associated with his
operations and above all he cares about each customer. His secrets
are all in this book. We should be grateful he has shared them with us.'
*Donald R. Keough, President and Chief Operations Officer,
The Coca-Cola Company (USA)*

'It's a jewel.'
Ralph S. Larsen, Chairman and CEO, Johnson & Johnson

FEARGAL QUINN

MIND YOUR OWN BUSIN€SS

SURVIVE AND THRIVE IN GOOD TIMES AND BAD

THE O'BRIEN PRESS
DUBLIN

First published 2013

by The O'Brien Press Ltd
12 Terenure Road East, Rathgar, Dublin 6, Ireland
Tel: +353 1 4923333 · Fax: +353 1 4922777
Email: books@obrien.ie · Website: www.obrien.ie

ISBN: 978-1-84717-547-2

British Library Cataloguing-in-Publication Data
A catalogue record for this title is available from the British Library

1 2 3 4 5 6 7 8 9 10
13 14 15 16 17 18 19 20

Layout and design by the Little Red Pen, Dublin
Printed and bound by Colorman (Ireland) Limited, Dublin
The paper used in this book is produced using pulp from managed forests.

Contents

Every morning in Africa, a gazelle wakes up. It knows it must run faster than the fastest lion or it will be killed.

Every morning a lion wakes up. It knows it must outrun the slowest gazelle or it will starve to death.

It doesn't matter whether you are a lion or a gazelle: when the sun comes up, you'd better be running.

(African proverb)

Preface

One day back in the 1950s, I accompanied my father to a grocery shop in Dun Laoghaire. We got chatting to the grocer,
and my father asked him, 'How are things?'

'Very tough,' the grocer explained. 'It's not like it was in
the old days. You know it's really very tough nowadays.'

When we came out from the shop, my father turned to
me and said, 'You know that's exactly what my own father
heard people say back in the 1930s.'

More than twenty years later, during the 1970s, I rather
innocently asked another shop owner how business was
going.

'Ah, I think I got into the business at the wrong time,
it's not like it was in the old days – it's particularly tough,'
was his reply.

Clearly, some things never change!

Over more than fifty years as a retailer, I have been lucky to learn at first hand what it takes to thrive in business, whether times are good or bad. Also I know from experience that in order for any business to prosper, it has to be firmly rooted in fertile ground.

And for this to happen, everybody involved in the enterprise has to be willing to continuously and relentlessly work the land to ensure it remains fresh and nutritious.

Yet, instead of proactively addressing their problems head on, I believe the type of negative thinking that my father and I saw in Dun Laoghaire (and that his father before him witnessed) has once again taken hold in many businesses.

Make no mistake: it can be very easy to give in to the temptation of believing that we're not going to succeed, because the marketplace is just not fair out there.

The truth is that you can talk yourself into believing just about anything in business, if you really want to. And, believe me, this can be a very seductive, and ultimately destructive, proposition.

One of the reasons I have written this book is because I am convinced this has simply got to change.

This book is aimed at people who own their own business and those who hope to own their own business one day. I also hope it will be of assistance to the very many people who work for an existing business and desperately want to help improve its prospects.

The idea for this book came from two very different, if complementary, sources.

The first catalyst was when I turned to Denise, my wife, in frustration one day about three years ago. I had been watching the evening news in front of the fire, and all of the reports were focused in one way or another on the terribly gloomy economic situation in the world today.

'You know, I really feel for those people out there struggling to pay their mortgages, and for the business owners who are worried if they will have to shut up shop,' I said. 'But we also have to move beyond this ... because I just know that recession can be a good thing for businesses, too.

'If only they could learn how to put excellence at the heart of everything they do. If they can look after their own business, first and foremost, then they can give themselves every chance of prospering no matter what the economic climate.'

Now, my dear wife had heard my opinions on this topic before and was not about to let me expand on them (again!). She turned to me and said, 'Feargal, I know how passionate you are about this. But every time you see a depressing news report on the television, which, let's face it, is pretty much all of the time these days, you get upset. It has got to the stage where I can't bear to watch the 9 o'clock news with you because I know something is going to set you off! If you feel so strongly why don't you do something about it?'

And I knew she was right. Because the truth is that the similarities between today's economic climate and when I started out in business back in 1960 are uncanny.

Back then, emigration and unemployment were also rife in Ireland, and the government of the day had great difficulty balancing its budgets. Like today, people had very little money to spend, and access to credit was very difficult to come by.

In fact, in many ways economic life was even tougher then than it is now. However, there was one major difference between the early 1960s and nowadays.

In those days, Ireland was always in recession, yet we never thought in this way! The term 'recession' was not part of our collective mentality as we knew nothing else other than tough economic times.

Crucially, this meant that in order to survive and prosper it was important to just get on with things.

In my case, this included persevering with my rather ambitious plan to open my first shop. My father served as Chairman of the company. It was called Quinn's Supermarket, situated on a large site in Clanbrassil Street, Dundalk, and opened on 25 November 1960.

I was convinced that grocery retailing was on the brink of a revolution, and I was determined to be amongst the leaders of that revolution in Ireland.

Because my business was forged during tough economic times, I was acutely conscious from day one of the need for my shop to truly excel if my fledgling business was to have any chance of surviving.

I knew it simply had to offer something different from its competitors — and something better, too.

This fear of being 'ordinary' served as a powerful motivator throughout my business career. It became, if you like, a sort of internal motto for me as we went on to build a successful supermarket company, Superquinn. It created thousands of jobs in the Irish retail sector before we brought new investors into the company and transferred ownership in 2005.

We achieved this success by truly valuing (or crowning) the customer, and putting the pursuit of excellence at the heart of everything we did.

The second inspiration for this book was my involvement in the *Feargal Quinn's Retail Therapy* television programme, which airs on RTÉ television.

During each episode of the series, I visited a different struggling retail outlet. Over time, I helped them to identify where they could improve and worked with them to plot a way out of their difficulties.

As I visited the businesses that featured in the show, I was amazed to see many of the same issues rearing their heads time and again.

Among the recurring themes I encountered were the importance of truly valuing your customers, staff and suppliers; why it is so vital to come out of denial and to make time to see the wood for the trees; and the need to properly plan for succession in family-owned businesses.

Elsewhere, I saw just how important it is to do the simple things well, such as making a good first impression on customers and ensuring none of them feel alienated, while at the same time fostering a culture of innovation based on really listening to their needs.

Working alongside the programme participants, ultimately we succeeded in addressing the things that were holding them back, meaning their businesses could be put on a sound footing.

My involvement in the series got me thinking: wouldn't it be great if we could find a way to help others learn from the mistakes of our show participants, and to avoid the obvious pitfalls in business?

A sort of handbook of what not to do during a recession – for want of a better phrase!

With Denise's call to action ringing in my ears, and my experiences with the *Feargal Quinn's Retail Therapy* participants as another source of inspiration, one evening I sat down and started writing out my thoughts on how businesses facing challenges during a recession can look to renew themselves.

This book represents the culmination of these early efforts.

I have tried to use real-life examples from my own career, as well as from my experiences with the *Retail Therapy* series, to illustrate the kinds of problems I have seen over and over again.

Although the television programme focuses on the (very) personal stories of those who generously have agreed to take part, the themes involved are universal.

Every issue we found with individual case studies is, I believe, being replicated ten times over elsewhere. And often in a much more serious fashion.

Where possible, I have tried to show how these pitfalls can be either avoided in the first place or tackled head on.

I truly hope readers of this book will find useful, practical tips that easily can be applied to any business situation.

What I will not do, however, is to claim I have all the answers. I do not. Your customers do, which is why you may have noticed I have not offered readers a money-back guarantee!

I would like to dedicate this book to two sets of people. The first set of people you can probably guess: they are each and every one of the participants in the series. They deserve my most sincere thanks for allowing me to hold a mirror up to business practices today.

In so doing, they were incredibly open and honest and displayed a commitment to change that is truly inspiring.

It is by no means an exaggeration to say that without their willingness to allow themselves to face such intense (and very public) scrutiny this book would never have been written. If in some small way their experiences can serve to help others, then they will have done their fellow entrepreneurs some service.

Indeed, nothing would give me greater pleasure in years to come than to hear that even one extra person had a full-time job because their employer took the time to read about their experiences here.

In my role as a public representative, and more recently while travelling around Ireland with my television series, I have witnessed at first hand the effect the current economic climate is having on people on the ground. Yet there remains a powerful, almost palpable drive to succeed among the people I meet on a daily basis.

This second set of people is a constant source of hope and inspiration to me.

I would like to dedicate this book to these people – and the many like them who are willing to do whatever it takes to truly excel in business.

Set the tone

Learn to lead by example

....

The very dignified gentleman who approached me in the hotel car park was unmistakable. The former President of Ireland, Dr Patrick Hillery, had been studying me intently from a distance, without my knowing it.

I had been absent-mindedly picking up some litter outside the Marine Hotel in Sutton, across the road from the Superquinn Support Office, when the President spied me.

'I used to do the same, at the Áras, you know. If I saw a piece of litter I would go around and pick it up myself. And if I saw another bit a little further away, and another a bit further on I would pick them up too. Then I got ticked off

....

by the security and the Áras staff. They told me I didn't need to do it because I was the President.'

Of course, like the Áras, the Marine Hotel employed people to look after litter in its outside areas too.

So why on earth was I picking up the litter?

An American friend of mine, Fred Meijer, had a big supermarket chain in Grand Rapids, Michigan, until he passed away in 2011 at the grand old age of ninety-one.

Some years previously, a group of us went to see him, and he showed us around. Fred was probably in his eighties at the time.

His father Hendrik was a barber with a small grocery shop above his salon, and his mother started off selling groceries too. In the 1940s, when Fred decided to go into business with his father, they started selling groceries on a larger scale.

Fred was a true innovator, and the quintessential self-made man.

In the 1960s he was the first to introduce the concept of the hypermarket, combining a grocery store with a general discount merchandise store, to the USA. It was a model that would subsequently be copied by Sam Walton, founder of the giant Walmart chain, amongst others.

In time, the company successfully expanded, until it became a major regional employer. With over 200 stores and more than 170 gas stations in Michigan, Ohio, Indiana, Illinois and Kentucky, Fred Meijer's company continues to handle its business based on the simple philosophy of Fred's father, Hendrik. This was to 'Take care of your customers, team members, and community … And all of those will take care of you, just like a family.'

It is not a coincidence that the company's slogan to this day is 'Higher Standards, Lower Prices', while its motto since its foundation in 1934 is 'Customers don't need us, we need them.'

As we went around his warehouse during our visit, I asked Fred various questions about his way of doing business. At that stage, the company had 170,000 employees.

I asked him about the intricacies of how his delivery trucks worked. His response remains with me to this day.

'Feargal, I don't know. When a company gets this big, sometimes all I can do is set the tone.'

Fred was true to his word on this, in everything he did. As we went around his shops together, Fred never parked in a good car parking space; he always parked at the back of the car park and walked up to the entrance.

He never walked up without wheeling a couple of shopping carts with him. He never walked past a piece of litter or paper on the floor, even in the car park, without picking it up (much like President Hillery and me).

And he never walked past one of his own employees without shaking hands with them, even though he couldn't possibly know them all personally with such a huge number of people working there.

With his customers, he was known for giving out Fred Meijer-branded 'Purple Cow Coupons', redeemable for a free ice-cream cone, to remind them he was personally grateful for their custom.

I was thoroughly impressed with all of this, to such an extent that I even copied him by handing out doughnut cards of my own.

Because essentially what he was doing was setting the tone that he wanted others within his company to follow. He was leading by example in the most wonderful way.

And it was fairly clear when you went to his competitors, despite the fact that they might have given just as good value, or had similar goods for sale, there was something missing.

They were not Fred Meijer!

More often than not, the overall tone of a company is set by the boss of the company. But this can have both positive and negative implications at times.

A few years ago, I was packing customers' bags at a Superquinn checkout and a man came up to me. I asked, 'Is everything OK?' and he said 'Hmmmm.' Sensing there was something on his mind, I asked him to tell me more.

He explained that when he was at the butcher's counter, he was upset to see knives being left in a wash hand basin. The sink had a sign over it saying, 'This basin is for hand washing only.'

I said, 'Oops, that's an error. It was quick of you to notice.'

'Well, I'm a quality-control inspector in the construction industry. I notice slippage of standards,' he responded.

Seizing the opportunity to pick his brains, I asked him, 'What's the most important thing in maintaining standards?'

He replied straight away: 'If the boss thinks it's important!'

And he was absolutely right.

In fact, earlier in the day, I had gone to that same butcher's counter to check on how it was doing. I had noticed a damaged package that I withdrew, and I noticed a customer being kept waiting, so I ensured she was looked after.

But I had missed the unhygienic knives in the wash hand basin.

The truth was that, for whatever reason, I had not put the storage of those knives high on the agenda when it came to our butcher's counter.

And, because of my attitude, the manager of the shop, who had responsibility for 300 employees, also didn't place it high on his priority list when it came to ensuring standards.

In turn, his butchery department manager didn't make it a priority, meaning his thirty or so staff at the counter did not deem it of importance either.

Without knowing it, as the boss I was setting the poor standard that was being followed by the shop manager: if I wasn't putting something high on the agenda, then my employees didn't either.

This was a very important lesson for me to learn. By giving an example to his or her employees, the boss of any business, no matter how big or small, sends out an important message. It is this: 'This is how I want our company and our employees to behave. See, look to me for your lead.'

If, for example, a boss is surly or uninterested because he or she is stressed out by the recession, or is perhaps overly aggressive in their approach to business dealings, this will transmit itself to his or her senior managerial colleagues and right the way down through the organisation.

But when the tone is right it permeates throughout the company in a much more positive way. And, as in the case of Fred Meijer, it can lead to a distinct competitive advantage, too.

Another way of describing the tone of a company is the culture and the values that its leaders instil in their employees.

Once, during a visit to Japan, I was invited to the opening of a department store. We were invited in before the shop opened. The chairman, the managing director and all senior managers arrived down to the shop floor. There they met with the heads of each department.

You could see, right around this department store, with probably a few hundred employees, groups of managers huddled around getting the message that the general manager or chairman had for them at 8.30 a.m.

The manager of each department then gathered his or her team around them at 8.45 a.m. They were given the message for the day, a different one each day, which helped define the tone in-store. Then in turn they spread the message to their own staff.

They opened the doors at 9 a.m., and everybody inside – the chairman, the managing director and all the other managers – began welcoming the customers as they came

> By giving an example to his or her employees, the boss sends out an important message: 'This is how I want our company and our employees to behave. See, look to me for your lead'.

in with these messages still fresh in the employees' ears.

Clearly, they were setting an example. And I was amazed to hear this happened every day in every shop. Because of this, the opening of the shop each morning had become an important occasion for management, staff and customers alike.

It is a brilliant example of how to ensure that everyone in your company is delivering the same message, from the bottom up, while also showing your customers just how much you value their business.

The tone within a business can manifest itself in some surprising ways, too.

If I had my way, anyone devising a sign would be required by law to have handle with care printed on their arm to remind them!

This is because the language and tenor of the signs you use around your shop can reveal a lot more about your business than you may wish. I have to sheepishly admit that is not something we always got right at Superquinn.

Some years ago, a small number of people were abusing the free parking we offered in the car park in Blackrock. So we put in a new sign that said, 'After two hours there will be a charge of £1 per hour to park.'

The aim was to encourage only our customers to use the car park. But the sign we used was badly worded, leading to an outcry from the very people we wanted to entice in. We responded quickly, by changing the tone of the sign, but not the policy behind it.

Instead, it now said, 'The first two hours are free.'

As I say, we had not changed the thinking behind the sign one bit. But the way we expressed the sentiments was much less aggressive. Importantly, it was also far more in keeping with the image and tone we wanted to portray in our company.

Over the years, we also had many problems with the signs at our express checkouts, which were supposed to help customers get through the tills quickly. Being honest, we could never make a sign that didn't cause rows!

Invariably, some customers would complain if they saw others with more than the ten permitted items using this lane and would wonder why our staff did not refuse to serve them at this particular till. It was, after all, supposed to be reserved for customers who had only a small amount of shopping.

But it is also quite difficult for a checkout operator or supervisor to say to a customer who has been queuing up for three or four minutes, 'Oh, sorry, this is the wrong queue.' And, of course, we hated having to tell any customer looking to buy goods in our shop that they could not give us their money!

This is where a small tweak to the tone of our signs worked wonders. Instead of saying the express lane was only for ten items or under, we saw how in America some stores said 'About ten items.'

We changed the signs in our shops to say, 'This lane is reserved for customers with about ten items' and made sure they were large and very visible.

The new policy meant that customers had some leeway to go up to eleven or twelve items in the express queue without prompting the indignation of their fellow customers.

The results were immediate, so much so that it became a rare event to have somebody go through with twenty items, causing a problem.

When we eventually decided to introduce coin-operated trolleys at our Superquinn shops, we did so very reluctantly. We felt it was a disadvantage for customers to have to fish around for the change they needed. But eventually we simply could not avoid following suit.

What really surprised me was the reaction of some local businesses to the move.

One shop put three signs on their window, saying bluntly, 'No change for trolleys given here.'

In the face of this resistance, we stationed a trolley host with change next to our trolleys, and later with tokens, to get around the problem. Yet I still couldn't get over the fact that the shopkeeper had put three big signs up.

One day, my curiosity got the better of me. I became so perplexed that I marched into the shop and asked the shopkeeper behind the counter, 'Would you not be better coaxing people in rather than having these negative signs in your window?'

'It is an awful nuisance having people coming in here, we are busy and we have to spend all our time giving change,' was the curt response.

To my dismay, I discovered that in some of our other shopping centres, the same thing happened, with a number of shops putting similarly worded signs up. I felt, and still do feel, these businesses were seriously shooting themselves in the foot with this approach.

But Hugh Crilly, in the Blackrock hardware shop, adopted a far more positive attitude. He put up a positive sign saying, 'We are happy to give you change for your trolleys.' Hugh told me he had worked out that people coming into his shop for change would invariably see something they wanted to buy.

He was seizing the opportunity that coin-operated trolleys had presented, in order to make more money!

And, needless to say, he made sure that the customers who frequented his shop looking for change came away with a very positive image of his business, too.

Of course, no matter what tone or wording you use, some signs simply need to be taken away and thrown in the dustbin!

I saw a sign up in a shop one time that said, 'The fish we sell tomorrow is still in the sea.'

Inspired, we proudly put up our own version in one of our supermarkets. It said, 'The eggs we sell tomorrow are still in the hen.'

Our customers soon let us know they did not appreciate

this reminder of just where their eggs came from! And that sign was gone within a matter of days.

2

Dare to be different

*Being extraordinary means
being willing to break
from the 'done thing'*

....

It might seem strange nowadays, but back in the 1960s shops in Ireland typically had littered floors.

It was the 'done thing' in all shops. Everybody just threw their rubbish on the floor, knowing that somebody else would eventually be around to brush it up.

I saw a man in our Walkinstown shop going to smoke a cigarette. He took the last cigarette out and just dropped the packet on the floor. I picked it up and said, 'Ah, I think you dropped something.'

....

He said, 'No, no, thanks, I have just finished with it.'

In other words, it didn't even dawn on him that you don't just drop things. Clearly he just dropped it because there were other things on the floor. In the middle of a food shop!

Even the employees, when they were opening packages, left the discarded wrapping on the shop floor.

This seriously bothered me. I went to America in 1961, and I couldn't get over the fact that there were spotlessly clean floors in the supermarkets there.

But I worried it was so ingrained in the culture of the shopping experience in Ireland that it would be impossible to change it here. I would say to the staff, 'Excuse me, why is this stuff being left on the floor?' and the response I would get was 'Oh, it's OK, we are going to sweep it up afterwards.'

When I came back from America, I tried my best to keep the floors clean. But I couldn't make it work. In spite of my best efforts, people just kept dropping litter on the ground inside the shop.

I was attempting to set a new tone for our company, and I was continually coming up against a brick wall. But then something truly extraordinary happened that changed all this.

Paddy Keaveney, our manager in Blanchardstown, went on a study trip we organised to America. He came back and said to me, 'Feargal, I can't believe that everywhere in America there are clean floors. Nobody drops anything on the floor.'

Mind Your Own Business

We were competing in the Irish Quality Association awards that year. It had been won by a factory in Cork virtually every year previously. There was no chance that a supermarket could win the Hygiene Award because a factory could be spotlessly clean with twenty or forty people working in it, as opposed to a supermarket with upwards of 150 staff and thousands of customers.

In addition, supermarket staff and customers were all too accustomed to littering the shop floor.

But Paddy Keaveney came back from America a man possessed.

It was coming up to Halloween in Blanchardstown, and he took his team of young workers out into the shop car park. These were the young fellows who swept the floor with special big brushes. And he organised a bonfire of the brushes!

He put petrol on the bonfire, and they threw all the sweeping brushes onto the fire, while we proclaimed, 'We are not going to sweep the floor ever again!' and we all drank a celebratory Coca-Cola.

I have to admit, I thought Paddy was a little bit mad.

But because Paddy said, 'We are not going to let the first piece of litter ever get to the floor,' it changed the tone in the shop almost overnight. The example we took was if you go into your own drawing room you don't drop something on the floor.

If it is midnight, and there's been a party in your drawing room, and everyone is around with streamers and beers and bottles and things, you have no bother dropping something on the floor because everything else is there.

Paddy's point was if we didn't let the first piece get to the floor then we wouldn't have a problem.

It was a hard-line 'zero tolerance' approach to litter. And do you know what?

Within two weeks the supermarket's floors were clean. Not because we swept them, but because we didn't allow anything get to the floor in the first place.

Our employees no longer threw things on the floor. If you did drop something, you picked it up. If a customer dropped something, it was picked up within seconds.

And because people don't drop things on clean floors, our customers soon stopped doing so too. Within two weeks, every Superquinn shop had clean floors.

I imagine Marks & Spencer had clean floors, but there were no Marks & Spencer shops in Ireland in those days. But certainly, our competitors – Quinnsworth, H. Williams, the others who were there – all had untidy floors.

By introducing this new policy on cleanliness within our shops, we knew we were setting a very different tone. Suddenly customers could see when they walked into a Superquinn that we had clean floors, unlike our competitors.

We won the Hygiene of the Year Award – the first time anybody other than a factory had won it.

And within months we were being followed by our competitors. I had been to the States and had seen clean floors. But I didn't find the formula to solve it, despite being the boss of the company.

But Paddy Keaveney did!

I tell this story because I am convinced any company that is really serious about standing out during a recession needs to be willing to challenge the accepted business norms from time to time. They need to not just do the 'done thing'.

This can be a very difficult thing to do because it can require the introduction of a radical new tone that flies in the face of conventional marketplace standards.

Also, it is not always possible for the owner of a business to personally introduce a new tone to a company.

As I learned from Paddy Keaveney, very often they need to rely heavily on the support of their colleagues if they are going to achieve this. Let me give you another example of just what I mean.

When we opened our Blackrock shop in 1984, anyone could smoke inside a supermarket while doing their shopping.

People were thought to be more relaxed if they could smoke when they came in to shop, and, as one person put it to me, 'Everybody expects to be able to smoke in a supermarket.'

One day, my colleague Pat Kelly, regional manager, came to me with a radical proposal.

'Let's ban smoking in our shops,' he said.

Pat felt there was a strong case to be made for ensuring our shops were smoke-free, particularly as we were in the fresh-food business. And, I have to say, I agreed with him.

Because I felt it was the right tone for our company's shops, I said to Pat, 'OK, let's do it.'

It was not an easy decision to make. I even remember a customer saying to me, 'If you don't let me smoke when I'm shopping I'm not coming in here again.'

Now, no shopkeeper likes to hear this from a customer. But I was convinced, on balance, that more people would be pleased than dissatisfied at a smoking ban in our shops, including parents fearful of their young children breathing in second-hand smoke.

I didn't find a problem saying to our customers, 'We are in the food business and smoking doesn't fit in.'

I said, 'I'm sure we are doing the right thing.' And we went ahead and banned smoking. For the reasons outlined above, our signage didn't just say 'No smoking.'

Instead, the tone we adopted was far less confrontational. The signs said 'Thank you for not smoking!' And it was the subtle twist in the wording that made a difference.

We set a new standard in May 1984 when we opened our Blackrock shop with a smoking ban. The tone we wanted to adopt was that this is a food shop and we are not going to accept smoking.

Really, we were leading the way in this. What's more, we were willing to say we believe the customer is (nearly) always right, but to the customer who smokes in our shop — unfortunately you are not right.

Why? Because it was against the tone we wanted to set for Superquinn.

If you set the right tone for your company, there can be other less obvious but equally important benefits.

Throughout my working life, I found the culture and tone within Superquinn played a key role in attracting and retaining the best quality employees for the company.

Of course, particularly during a recession, you are always going to have people who come to work with you because they just need a paying job that puts food on their family's table.

But over the years generally I have found the people who stayed with me tended to share my values and my approach to doing business. Often they worked their way up in the company, meaning they had a keen sense of the culture of Superquinn from an early age.

In other words, this helped to instil in them a belief in what we were trying to achieve with our family business. And if they bought into our approach they could potentially go on to progress through the company's management structures.

This is a very powerful message to convey to talented colleagues. It is worth remembering that these are the very people every struggling business needs to retain if it is to succeed during a major economic downturn.

Of course, as in the case of both Paddy Keaveney with his brushes and Pat Kelly with his cigarette ban, the culture of the company needed to allow them to 'think outside the box' by floating new ideas that challenged the accepted norms.

It is also important that companies bring in outsiders from time to time in order to challenge its internal thinking and beliefs.

But the important point here is that the people who grow up in a business invariably assimilate the tone set by the boss.

So you had better work darned hard at making sure you have set it right.

This leads me to another key way in which a business leader can help to set the tone: humour.

3

Ah, go on, humour me

Why having fun makes good business sense

....

Some years ago, I was sitting with Denise in the lounge of O'Hare Airport in Chicago waiting for a connecting flight. We decided to order a bite to eat. When we went to order a glass of wine to accompany our meal – the drinking age there is twenty-one or over – we were more than a little taken aback by the response we received from the waitress.

'I would love to serve you alcohol today, Sir, but I'm afraid it is company policy to ask anyone who may not be of drinking age for identification. Do you have some ID on you?' she asked cheekily.

I like to think I have a youthful face, but we were, and are, the parents of grown-up children!

The waitress was being serious, but I found it just hilarious. And I have used her approach on the shop floor ever since, because in Superquinn we had a rule that you have to be twenty-five to buy alcohol.

I get a particular buzz going up to the older man or woman on the shop floor with a bottle of wine in their basket and saying, 'Excuse me, but are you over twenty-five? May I see your ID?' Invariably I get a hug from the ladies!

I do this for a very specific reason: if the boss is willing to greet customers with a sense of humour, no matter how busy or pressurised he or she is, it's very likely to rub off on the rest of the staff too. And a smiling customer is a contented customer!

One of the great advantages I had in life was that I grew up in a holiday camp. The reason I say this is because effectively it meant I grew up in show business. And, in some respects, because of this, I have felt always there is a link between being a retailer and entertainment.

If a retailer can have that touch of show business about them, then they will continually challenge themselves to come up with something new to keep the customer – their audience – entertained. 'Why would somebody come to our theatre (our shop) next week unless we have something new to show them?' is a question I would often ask myself.

If you want to stand out from your competitor, there are few better ways of doing so than by injecting a sense of fun into your company.

But first of all you must have the basics right.

You may succeed in creating great excitement and a lot of atmosphere in your shop or business, but when someone comes to you for your service, they need to know that you remain focused on diligently serving their needs to the best of your ability.

If the boss is willing to greet customers with a sense of humour, no matter how busy or pressurised he or she is, it's very likely to rub off on the rest of the staff too

This is what I like to call doing the 'boring' stuff … brilliantly! If, for example, you have run out of the particular brand of butter or sugar your customer wants, or your pricing is way out of line because you have taken your eye off the ball, then you are in serious trouble regardless of what you do to entertain them.

I vividly remember a customer coming up to me in our Finglas shop one day. We were having great fun staging a 'Win Your Weight in Groceries' competition in-store. This was run in conjunction with some of our suppliers and involved individually placing some lucky competition winners on a plank over a barrel, while crowds watched us fill the other side with groceries until it balanced. (We obviously hoped for our contestants to be as thin as possible!)

As you can imagine, this was prompting loud cheering among the assembled watching crowds. But just then a woman came over to bend my ear.

Expecting her to talk about how much fun this was, I was more than a little bit taken aback when she said, 'I wish there were times when you weren't entertaining us and just got on with providing us with groceries. Everyone here is too busy focusing on the entertainment. I won't be shopping here again if this doesn't change.'

And do you know what? She was right. Not everyone wants to be entertained all of the time when they come in to do their shopping, so it is important to ensure that one is not sacrificed for the other.

There is a lovely ancient Chinese proverb that has always struck me as hitting the nail on the head. It says:

A man without a smiling face must not open a shop.

This refers to retailing specifically, but it could just as easily apply to every type of business activity.

Throughout my working career, I have always made sure to wake up in the morning really looking forward to coming to work, excited about the fun that the day will bring.

Likewise, I have tried, and hopefully succeeded, to imbue this same sense of anticipation and good humour in my staff. Of course there are times when all businesses become stressed. But it is hugely important, particularly during a recession, not to let the weight of financial and other pressures bear too heavily on the mood of both management and staff.

Again, we are back to the 'tone'. If the staff is transmitting a stressed or negative vibe to one another or, even worse, to their customers, then this is going to impact negatively on trade. Nobody wants to do business with surly, uninterested or just plain bored workers.

Over the course of the *Feargal Quinn's Retail Therapy* television series, we came across retailers who, on occasion, seemed to have lost the simple joy of coming to work. There were many reasons for this, including financial, emotional and physical stress.

But the net result was the same: they no longer looked forward to starting their working day. In many cases, the lack of energy and vitality this generated had transmitted itself to their staff too, meaning there was little or no sense of dynamism or enthusiasm in their businesses. What was good enough for their boss was good enough for them!

Frequently, this corrosive sense of unhappiness was also reflected in the personality of their business: namely, dull, unimaginative decor and cluttered, poorly conceived layout and display areas.

Yet, in my experience, if you can motivate yourself to entertain people when they come to your shop and choose to view your job through a positive, rather than constantly negative, lens, this can provide a powerful energising force.

This can have a major positive impact on your staff, too, who will invariably see your approach to work and normally follow your lead (or tone).

Of course, it is not easy to be positive all of the time, and some people are inherently more upbeat than others. But, as a leader of a business, I cannot stress enough just how important it is to set aside any personal feelings you might have in order to focus on portraying a positive attitude to your staff and customers.

In my experience, this can often become a self-fulfilling prophecy: once you decide to be more positive, good things can and do happen!

This is one reason why I have always thought it must be difficult to be an undertaker. It is perhaps the one job where you can't really bounce into work proclaiming, 'Oh, sorry about your difficulty, but did you hear the one about the …?'

Generating goodwill amongst your customers by creating a sense of fun and excitement can also be a great way of differentiating yourself from your competitors. This does not necessarily mean you have to put on an elaborate or expensive show every time they come into your shop.

For example, if there is a particularly cold spell, offering free soup, tea or coffee to customers as they enter your shop is a really simple way of showing you value the effort they have made to bring you their business.

By talking to your suppliers and telling them what you want to do, more often than not it should also be possible to arrange a discount so the cost of providing these treats is minimised.

Just like Fred Meijer with his ice-cream-cone vouchers, we often sought to surprise our customers and spread some good humour. At one stage, we even gave out free goldfish to Superquinn customers!

Clearly we just wanted to do something nice for our customers, without expectation of any great reward in terms of its immediate impact on our day-to-day profits. But the beauty of this approach is that, by demonstrating in little ways just how much your customer means to you, you are also creating a buzz around your shop.

If someone leaves your shop talking about the free treat they got, then chances are they will spread the word to others. This is invaluable when it comes to generating positive word of mouth.

At the back of your mind, it is hugely useful to constantly ask yourself, 'Is there something or other I can do that will have people go back home and say, "Gosh, do you know what happened to me today? Do you know where I was?"'.

And the financial cost of this brilliant advertising?

Pretty much nada.

Zilch!

Nothing!

ᚱᚪᚔᚲ!

Putting a smile on somebody's face can truly work wonders in a business situation. It always amazes me that companies do not do it more.

At this stage, I want to let you into a little secret: you can even use humour to greatly improve the overall standards in your business.

Some twenty years ago in Superquinn, we drew up a list of everyday items that seemed to disappoint customers, what we called 'goofs' that we felt were not acceptable to us as a company. But instead of sending a top-secret memo around to all of our staff, with 'CLASSIFIED' stamped all over it, do you know what we did?

We did the complete opposite. Far from brushing our weaknesses under the carpet, we decided to tell our customers all about them! We printed up big signs for the shops and a small note for customers' personal use, about the size of a credit card, which detailed some of our biggest potential pitfalls.

These were distributed to customers at all our shops, and they could refer to them as they went around the shop floor. The goof card stated, 'Tell us when we goof, and we'll give you 100 SuperClub (loyalty scheme) points.'

Among the typical examples of goofs we highlighted were:

- if we give you a wobbly trolley
- if you find that we've charged you more than our signage says
- if we run out of labels for the fruit and vegetable weighing scales
- if you find any product out of date
- if we are fifteen minutes late in doing our temperature watch
- if there are no bones available for your dog at the butchery counter
- if your birthday cake is not ready more than fifteen minutes later than you ordered it.

You might ask why on earth we would want to put our biggest failings up in glittering lights, for all of our customers (and potential customers) to see. Well, we took the view that by being upfront and honest with our customers about our willingness to highlight instances where our standards had slipped, we were achieving two key things.

First, we were helping to retain their trust by letting them know we were serious about acting upon our faults.

Second, we were telling them we were sufficiently confident in our processes and procedures that it would not bankrupt the company if they were all going to be rewarded for keeping an eye on our standards. And by doing so with a smile on our face we were creating a real 'win-win' situation for everyone.

The 'goofs' scheme was a brilliant success. What's more, it also had another very interesting effect: it saved us a lot of money.

By asking our customers to tell us where we 'goofed', we were essentially making thousands of quality-control inspectors out of them. For a comparatively small financial investment, our customers became our eyes and ears on our shop floors, pointing out to us where our standards had slipped.

At one stage, there was even a 'Goof Lady'. Mary, from Carlow, used to patrol our shops looking for goofs in order to get her free 100 SuperClub points. I still remember the sense of apprehension among some of my colleagues when she was spotted in one of our shops!

Oh, and the relief too when she told me she no longer visited our Naas shop because there wasn't enough money in it for her. This told us all that the staff there had raised their standards so much it was not worth her while going there anymore.

Of course, she was more than a little miffed by this improvement.

But, naturally, we were delighted!

4

Recession as opportunity

Avoiding 'Can't See the Wood for the Trees' Syndrome

One of the most rewarding aspects of my involvement in the *Feargal Quinn's Retail Therapy* television series is the opportunity it has given me to spend time with small local businesses around the country.

All too often I have encountered stressed-out owners, whose worries are multiplying due to the worst recession Ireland has ever seen.

This is a time when customers have very little money to spend. And those who do are increasingly price-conscious, meaning retail margins are cut to the bone. Understandably, many of the people I meet are worried about whether they have any future at all in business.

Yet, far from being a doom-and-gloom situation, I remain convinced the recession offers a brilliant opportunity for business owners – if they are willing to take it.

Now, I know you might be thinking Feargal Quinn has finally lost his marbles!

Gone loco!

Mad as a hatter!

In fact, as I write this, I'm pretty sure I've just seen my dog, Clouseau, looking at me a bit quizzically.

Surely a situation where people don't have money to spend – and will only do so if they can get a bargain – is the ultimate nightmare scenario for retailers.

What on earth do I mean?

There is no doubt that things are incredibly tough for a lot of people out there.

Not only have I witnessed this at first hand via my television programme, but I also see it in the faces of the people I meet on a daily basis through my work as a public representative. Yet I am certain this crisis can bring about positive changes in the way many businesses do things.

In order for this to happen, however, business people have to be willing to help themselves. They need to come out of their bunkers.

Tough times such as these can offer traders an invaluable opportunity to re-evaluate their businesses, with a view to getting the fundamentals right.

Among the questions they should be asking at moments like these are:

> I am certain this crisis can bring about positive changes in the way many businesses do things

- 'What am I doing right?'
- 'Am I really listening to my customers (and potential customers?)' and
- 'What do I need to change to make my business as relevant as possible to my customers?'

Unfortunately, the shock of a major recession may encourage some owner-managers to do the exact opposite. Instead of facing up to what is happening, they continue doing what they always did. Effectively, they retreat to their bunkers and hope against hope that everything will be OK.

Invariably, it is not.

There are a range of other factors that can have a major impact on your chances of remaining in business when times are tough. These include the extent of your existing debt levels as well as your access to cash flow, customers and credit.

But here is the beauty of really using the opportunity that a recession presents. It pushes you to see things as they actually are, rather than how you wish they might be.

I cannot overstate the importance of doing this in business.

When you face up to the reality of your situation, you are already in a far better position to plan for the future than if you simply run away and hide from the truth.

It can be a lot harder to do this than you might think. This is particularly true when there are strong emotional ties to a family business, which can cloud judgement.

By subjecting yourself to a long-overdue root-and-branch examination of your business model, you may even find that you decide to exit your company or close the business.

While painful, this too can be a good thing in the long term, particularly if it stops you running up more back-breaking debt by pumping money into an unsustainable enterprise.

On the other hand, if you can succeed in putting the basics of your business onto a sound footing, maybe for the first time in a long time, then you will give yourself every chance of securing your future as a successful enterprise.

And that is something you might never have 'got around' to doing if things were a bit easier, with customers and cash aplenty coming through your doors.

What's more, you will also be well placed to benefit from any potential upturn in the economy down the line. This is because you will have a fundamentally sound business model, which may not have been the case during the so-called good years.

To achieve this, business owners need to avoid what I call the **Can't See the Wood for the Trees Syndrome**. They simply must take the time to step away from their daily pressures to plan for the future.

I was reminded of this when I visited McGreal's Department Store in Edenderry during the *Retail Therapy* series. Frances McGreal is a committed businesswoman who was under huge financial strain, having taken over the business from her late father, Billy, four years earlier.

Throughout my travels around the country as part of my television programme, I have encountered stressed-out, exhausted owner-managers just like Frances.

Sometimes I feel like shouting at the top of my voice, 'When you are exhausted or stressed out, your ability to manage your business is diminished, because you are so tired you cannot see the wood for the trees.'

Of course, I don't actually do this.

But management in every business, large or small, has to take a step back and plan for the medium to long term. If they don't, there is a real risk there won't actually be any medium- or long-term future at all.

This is something I feel extremely passionate about.

Far too many retailers get to Sunday evening, take a read from the till and simply measure performance versus the previous week. Of course that doesn't tell you a whole amount, especially when you take seasonal variations into account.

This is why targets are critical for any serious business. You have to look at last year, decide on where you want the business to be for the next twelve months, and then plot that target for every week going forward. By doing this you are taking control of your fate and driving your business. In the absence of such targets, there is a real risk that you will start coasting, meaning you are simply reliant on whether customers spend with you or not.

But with targets in place you are forced to drive the business, and to drive yourself! Indeed, I would go so far as to say you simply cannot expect to run a business that is serious about sales growth without credible sales targets in place. You may not always hit these targets, but the very fact they exist helps your business to stay focused on its medium- to longer-term goals.

Having worked alongside her father for twenty-five years in the shop, Frances had undoubtedly served a long apprenticeship at McGreal's. During the good times, the 420-square-metre shop employed twenty or so employees, but this had been reduced to just nine employees since the recession kicked in.

According to her children, Frances was working seven days a week in the shop. During the programme she told me there were days of despair 'when you wouldn't want to come to the shop'.

She said she would sometimes come to the front door of the shop and park the car outside the door. She would just sit there and not go in because she didn't look forward to coming to work.

'The joy has gone out,' she confided to me at one stage.

This was something we desperately needed to fix.

When Frances inherited the business, she found her real love was for the purchasing side of things – sourcing stock for the shop.

And lots of it, it transpired!

The shop was an Aladdin's cave of stock, with jewellery, crystal, ornaments, household goods, curtains, fireplaces, lamps, baby clothes, furniture, stationery, electrical goods, a party section with helium balloons and banners and even children's swimming pools.

It soon became clear that, since her father's death, there wasn't quite the same enthusiasm for selling on the shop floor, without his being around to inspire Frances.

One customer came up to me and spoke enthusiastically about her father Billy. 'I couldn't walk past the shop without him coming out and coaxing me in!' she told me.

Meanwhile, footfall to the town centre, where McGreal's is located, had also dwindled since the recession hit. Coupled with this, the shop was facing increasing competition from larger retailers such as Lidl, Aldi, Dunnes and Tesco, all of which are located on the outskirts of Edenderry.

McGreal's marketplace had changed significantly, too. Where during the Celtic Tiger years the shop had been selling a lot of its merchandise to Polish and other Eastern European workers, the bottom had fallen out of this segment of the market as they returned home or simply stopped spending.

Demand for household and garden goods, which had previously been big sellers in her shop, had fallen off dramatically due to the collapse in the property market. Frances had to respond to this new reality, as it was simply not good enough for her to keep doing what she had always done.

Frances also 'did' everything in the shop. There was absolutely no delegation, none at all. Like many self-employed business people, she was spending so much time working 'in' her business that she was neglecting to work 'on' her business.

We suggested a number of concrete steps that we felt would help Frances to address her problems. First, as Lara Snider, our retail design and visual consultant, said on the programme, the shop needed to be more comfortable and relaxing for the customer. It needed to be somewhere peaceful they could go to get away from the world.

Second, the business did not have ready access to outside finance. Again, this is something that many businesses complain of in the current banking climate.

To get around this hurdle, I suggested a clearance sale to generate much-needed cash for a revamp of the shop. This would allow Frances to put the money raised into sourcing new stock as well as improving the layout and branding within the shop.

Even more importantly, I sought to give Frances a break from her worries by sending her to a spa for the day. My fear was that because she was under so much pressure she simply could not step back and see the wood for the trees.

This can happen to anyone in business. But you have to learn to manage stress as a business owner.

Even though I can honestly say I have loved every minute of my career, I also had to be acutely aware when stress was impacting on my ability to do my job properly.

For example, I would always try to drop in to one of our shops if I happened to be nearby on my way home in the evening. But I also learned to listen to Denise, who would say to me occasionally that I did not look great or looked a little tired.

I would invariably say, 'Ah yeah, but I haven't been in that shop for the last two weeks.' To which she would reply, 'Yes, but you are not going to do any good going in looking the way you do.'

I would listen to her advice but can't say, hand on heart, that I always followed it!

But she was right. I was doing no one any good if I was not in top form myself going into work.

In the case of Frances, she was probably wiser not to go into work some days than to turn up with stress written all over her face. This would invariably transmit itself negatively to those around her, including her employees, and perhaps her customers too.

That's why I took her to a spa: to show her there are times when you are better keeping away, and the shop will not collapse if you make this time for yourself.

One trip to a spa was clearly not going to change everything for Frances. But by sending her there we wanted to show her a new way of dealing with her problems that she could incorporate into her everyday business approach from then on.

She clearly needed to make time to see the bigger picture. No matter how busy or stressed things were, she had to prioritise giving herself some headspace to think clearly.

Put another way, she had to get off the hamster wheel and watch it spin for a while until it eventually slowed down and she could take stock.

As we set about preparing for the relaunch of McGreal's, it was simply wonderful to watch Frances relax more and grow into her role as an instigator of change in her business. Of course, many of her stresses remained. Our presence did not wipe away the strain that she was under overnight.

But by working with her on plans for the medium to long term, it soon became clear she was beginning to enjoy this process. Simply breaking with the old patterns of behaviour meant there was a new energy and vitality to her and to her shop.

I am happy to say that by the end of this process Frances could not wait to get into work. Her blocked potential had been unleashed in the most wonderful way.

At a time when other shops were putting the boards up, she set about renaming her family shop (to McGreal's Acorn and Oak), while energetically setting about the task of improving the stock and floor layout. In effect, what Frances and her team created was a brand-new shop, albeit with familiar faces behind the tills. It is now a must-visit place for anyone in the Midlands with an interest in gifts and home furnishings.

What I believe Frances's story illustrates is the importance of prioritising a sense of perspective by allowing yourself to see the wood for the trees. This is even more crucial when times are stressful, such as during a major economic downturn.

The trick is to realise that responding to the day-to-day demands of keeping afloat, while necessary, is unlikely to be enough to ensure survival in the medium to longer term.

At some stage, every struggling business owner has to find the time to take a step back to chart their way out in a pragmatic, creative manner.

This should ideally be done with the help of other trusted colleagues or business associates.

Sounds pretty simple, doesn't it?

It is!

5

Sometimes love just ain't enough!

Replacing perspiration with inspiration

....

The pressures of a major recession can force any business, young or old, to get stuck in a potentially lethal rut.

This is because, when faced with the financial pressures of a recession, they frequently fall into the trap of putting all their energy into simply keeping going.

However, in my experience, they would be well advised to focus just as much, if not more, on how to do things better.

They need to learn how to replace perspiration with inspiration.

....

When I first met twenty-seven-year-old Caroline Gardiner, she was working every waking hour lovingly tending to her shop, Carrie's Cakes.

A single mother of one, she had opened her bakery six months earlier in a burst of youthful enthusiasm. She had calculated that the town of Ennis in Co. Clare would embrace her idea of specialising in exquisitely made cupcakes and other bakery delights.

It was easy to warm to Caroline's passion for her profession. Her skill, diligently learned at catering college and further honed with training as a professional pastry chef, is clear for all to see.

There was one pretty big problem, however. Caroline's typical working day started at 3 a.m. and did not end until 6 p.m. that evening. And her reward for this remarkable dedication to her new business?

Well, despite these incredibly long hours, she was barely making ends meet.

In truth, the Caroline Gardiner I met when I first entered her shop looked absolutely exhausted. The singer Patty Smyth had it right, you know, in her famous song: 'Sometimes, love just ain't enough!'

Ennis has a substantial population. Therefore, Caroline should have had access to a relatively large number of customers. They should have been beating down her door to sample her wares – if she was doing her marketing right.

Even more importantly, they should have been spreading the word amongst their friends about just how good her bakery products really were – and, trust me, her products were truly delicious!

But for some reason this was just not happening. I could see Caroline was clearly a born baker (if a pretty tired one). I had to ask myself the fundamental question: is she a born businesswoman too?

The initial signs were not encouraging. In her eagerness to open her business Caroline had signed a three-year lease that financially tied her to the property for all of that time.

This remained in force regardless of whether or not she stayed in business, meaning she could not afford to go under.

Another source of concern was the fact that her bakery shop was not offering freshly baked bread. This was something that had been a key factor in the Superquinn success story, as it allowed us to stand out from our competitors by trading on the uniqueness and freshness of our products.

I felt that by providing freshly baked bread Caroline could have a similar chance to differentiate herself from her competitors in the town.

But Caroline's problems did not end there. She was not displaying her products in the shop window, so people had little or no idea what she was offering. Once inside the shop, if a customer ever got that far, there were no clear price labels or descriptions of her products. It was as if customers were expected to engage in a guessing game if they wanted to actually buy anything.

There was also a real lack of any wow factor in the shop. Caroline needed to offer something that would make people remember Carrie's Cakes and leave them enthusiastically planning their next visit. There was little that would serve to separate her from the many other bakeries in the town.

As part of our research, we visited two of these and found they both had cupcakes. But whereas this formed only part of their overall offering, Caroline's focus seemed to be primarily on cupcakes, to the exclusion of practically everything else. There would need to be a pretty strong demand for cupcakes in the town of Ennis for the shop to trade successfully. Was this rather specialist product really so popular?

Meanwhile, she came in at 3 a.m. to get her baking done before the shop opened. By 10 a.m. there was little or no tantalising bakery smell in her shop.

Caroline should have been using the aroma of fresh baked goods to engage her customers' sense of taste and smell. Instead, customers were given no clue as to how delicious her goods were.

There was no branding on her cake boxes. This meant she was missing a golden opportunity for free advertising.

Perhaps most worrying of all was the fact that Carrie's Cakes was very much a one-woman operation. As a result, Caroline could not afford to get sick as there was no one else employed to take over the reins in her absence.

The business was completely reliant on her perspiration – not her inspiration!

Overall, I got a palpable sense that Caroline had focused all of her energy on getting the doors of her dream bakery open. Now her focus was on keeping them open, by dint of sheer hard slog.

But it simply was not working, so something had to be done. What was needed here was strategic thinking. We needed to formulate a coherent plan to help Carrie's Cakes survive. Otherwise I feared it would be curtains for the business.

There were many challenges facing Carrie's Cakes. But there were a number of positives too that gave me real hope for its future as a going concern. One huge plus was Caroline herself. Finding herself in a financially vulnerable position and unable to take any time off to simply step back and strategise for the future, she welcomed our arrival with open arms.

Far from being defensive when it came to suggested changes for her business, Caroline was remarkably open to new ideas. Also, we found that our arrival in itself prompted her to introduce some delightful changes of her own.

These included placing a bell outside the door of her shop so that customers would know that every time they heard the bell ring a fresh batch of bread was ready; putting a clock face with adjustable hands next to her cakes and pastries to show clients just when it had been baked; and installing a coffee machine to attract customers looking to linger for a cuppa and a chat over her products.

To get where she was in life, Caroline evidently had huge inner resources too. By virtue of her sheer drive and determination, she had kick-started her own personal development.

She had become the baker she was today only after undergoing years of dedicated training. This commitment to self-development is something that always gives me a huge buzz when I see it in an individual.

But now, in order to secure the future of her fledgling business, it was time to harness the same energy that had got her to this point in life. It would require her to make some pretty major decisions, too.

Throughout my years at Superquinn, the business came to a number of critical junctures in its development, times when, if the wrong decision was made, the future of the entire company could be placed in jeopardy.

One example that stands out was in 1982, when we were weighing up whether to build Blackrock Shopping Centre to house our new Superquinn shop. By any stretch of the imagination it was a huge decision for the company.

Owning and operating our own shopping centre, at a time when some of our advisers were suggesting there was not a big enough catchment area to make the business viable, would be a major departure for us.

We felt that the site, located at a key junction on the road leading out towards Dun Laoghaire and into Blackrock village, was too good to build just a stand-alone supermarket. Coupled with this, we had to make a judgement call on whether to build additional office space in Blackrock straight away.

Much like today, the early 1980s were a tough economic time for Ireland. There was the worry that the offices were likely to remain unoccupied for some years until the economy improved. As a result, they would not be generating any income for us, which is hardly an ideal situation for any business.

We had to make a decision. We had planning permission for a four-storey office block, and we were going to have to borrow a significant amount of money to build it. In the short to medium term, there was little prospect of a return on this investment.

We were also extending ourselves into property development, a business we knew little or nothing about. But if we did not build the office block, and we looked to do so in the future once the economy was in a healthier position, it would disrupt the whole shopping centre hugely.

I vividly recall going to our bank and showing them the map and our plans for the building. The banker said, 'There's an awful lot of sea there' – because of course on one side of Blackrock there is only sea! – 'You won't get many customers from that side.'

When I went back to see him, I brought with me a map of Sutton, where our Superquinn shop had been trading successfully for some years. And I (conveniently) pointed out there was far more sea to the north, south and east there than in Blackrock.

It was a massive decision for our company, and one I remember sweating over.

Ultimately, our move to open in Blackrock, office space and all, proved a great success.

I would be lying if I said I did not have sleepless nights, wondering if it was a good idea to expand. I was only too aware of the potential financial implications were it not to work out.

Yet I have always been a firm believer that if you don't believe enough in your business to invest *wisely* in it, then why on earth should your customers believe in your business too?

It is important to ask:

'Will this investment encourage people to drive past our competitors to our shop?'

'Will it coax them from surrounding areas, so that it becomes more than just a neighbourhood shop?'

'What do I have to do to get them to drive past my competitors?'

I emphasised the word 'wisely' above for a reason.

Any major decision has to be based on sound principles, including market research and analysis of the potential 'numbers' that any new development might add to your existing business (a cost–benefit analysis in management-speak).

There is also another, far more subtle but equally crucial element: your gut instinct. There have been times throughout my career when I have had to avoid the temptation to be overcautious. There have been times when I had to throw caution to the winds in order to progress the company.

This is never without risk. As with Blackrock, I was fortunate to get this right on many occasions.

But in other cases, I did not. The trick, of course, is to get more of the big decisions right than wrong, having weighed up all of the available evidence.

Carrie's Cakes was faced with a similar potentially game-changing decision. During the programme, we visited Ennis Engineering, where Gary Ennis gave us an insight into what might be possible in Caroline's shop.

> If you don't believe enough in your business to invest wisely in it, then why on earth should your customers believe in your business too?

By purchasing the right machinery, he showed us how she could not only diversify into bread-making for the first time but also reduce her own workload significantly.

This was because the machinery would allow her to make her dough in the evening, proof it overnight, and it would be ready to go in the morning. This was in marked contrast to her situation up until that point when she had to start baking from scratch at the crack of dawn.

On paper at least, it was a 'win-win' situation. The major snag was that Caroline needed to risk getting into more debt to help secure the future of her business.

Make no mistake, despite her enthusiasm, Caroline was under huge pressure: physical, emotional and financial. Truth was, the risks associated with failure were stressing her out.

Understandably, she worried greatly about money. She knew she was faced with a choice: she could continue to work long hours and see less of her lovely daughter Leah. Or she could invest in her business, improve her bakery offering and lessen her workload substantially.

One of the big questions Caroline had to ask herself was whether she could make a profit from the investment. She knew she would have to pay the interest on the money she would be borrowing from the bank for the next ten years.

She had to work out if she could make enough money from this investment to make it worthwhile.

Eventually, having weighed up the pros and cons of the equipment, Caroline decided to go ahead with the investment. And I am glad to report, from the front line, that since doing so she has hardly looked back.

Before the television programme featuring her was even transmitted her sales were up 50 per cent. I called her one day after the show went out, and she was so pleased she sounded giddy!

Since taking her strategic decision to invest in her business she told me she had never been so successful in her whole life. All of which success is running through her business, pumping life back into what is now a profitable going concern.

She had managed to succeed where many under-pressure businesses fail.

Instead of continuing to toil away at the coalface, desperately hoping that her energy and hard work would suffice, she had realised how important it was to stand back from her business and to plan for the future.

She had successfully replaced sheer perspiration with inspiration.

Oh, and she was finally getting some much-needed sleep, too.

6

Denial is not just a river in Egypt

Why doing nothing is not an option — keep calm, but don't carry on as before

....

We saw in Chapter 4 how Frances McGreal was so stressed out by the economic downturn that she was unable to gain the critical distance she needed to change her business for the better.

We worked with her to plan a path forward for her business, by taking the time to get some perspective on her situation. We were delighted to see her new approach gain real and tangible results.

There is one phenomenon that I see time and again in struggling businesses. It is something we touched upon earlier when we talked about the need to see the wood for the trees, but it is worth a more detailed exploration here.

This is the temptation to remain in denial about the real extent of your changed circumstances during a downturn. I use the word 'real' for a reason. Because unless you can learn to examine your business as it actually is, rather than as you imagine it to be, then you are in very serious trouble.

I first met Kim Buckley when I visited her shop as part of my television show. Kim runs a flower business, Liberty Florist, which has been passed down through the generations of her family.

Her great-grandmother Biddy McGrail was a well-known Dublin flower-seller in the 1800s, and Kim was working hard to maintain her family's legacy in the trade. However, times were extremely tough, and many businesses in the surrounding area, the Liberties of Dublin, had been forced to shut up shop.

Kim told me how, since the recession hit, she had been praying to her ancestor Biddy for help in overcoming her business problems.

As with Frances McGreal, one of the most striking things about Kim's business was the extent to which it was all on her shoulders – from buying flowers, to arranging them, to manning the shop, to doing the accounts and trying to drum up new business.

But, unlike Frances, who had other staff at her disposal

in her shop, Liberty Florist was a real one-woman operation. This left Kim with little time to engage in any structured planning for the future.

Although she had a business plan – to target the corporate market – she also lacked confidence in her ability to approach these potential clients. This was something we had to address urgently.

Kim had also made one major marketing error. There was no sign above her shop, so even if I was purposely looking for a shop called Liberty Florist it was a challenge to find it.

It goes without saying that every business owner or manager devotes a huge portion of their waking hours to their business. But if you cannot sell your service or product to others, then you are in a major difficulty from the start.

It was a theme that continued as I entered the shop. I looked in vain for information that reminded me I was not just in any shop but in Liberty Florist.

This is where branding and messaging play a huge role. If a bride looking for a good florist to decorate her pending nuptials is impressed by what she sees, then it is vital she comes away in no doubt as to where it was she saw this.

I also got the overriding sense that Kim, who is a very warm, engaging person, had given in to the temptation to retreat to her shop and to prioritise doing what she loved best – arranging flowers – when what she needed to do was to go out to promote herself and her business.

Kim was focused on using her talent for flower-arranging to put together lovely bouquets within the safe confines of her shop. It was as if she thought the very fact that she was keeping busy in the shop meant that customers would just walk through her door.

Unfortunately it just does not work that way. Every business person has to be continually thinking up new ways of attracting customers to sample their wares.

What is more, Kim was also struggling to deal with the financial reality of her situation, running a business that was barely staying afloat. She was very fearful about what the future held for her.

She told me how she would be overcome with fear and would question what she was doing.

I have to confess I had a lot of sympathy for Kim. To a certain extent I also understood why she was where she was.

But I cannot emphasise strongly enough that when times are tough, simply doing what used to work in the past is a recipe for disaster.

However much you may wish to, you can't stay shivering in your cave, hoping the world outside will leave you be.

While the temptation might be to batten down the hatches and remain in denial, it is vitally important to be able to react cleverly to external changes that impact on your business.

Some time before we visited the shop, a bus stop had been moved from outside Kim's shop. This meant that Kim's ready access to people either waiting for a bus or alighting from one no longer existed.

But when I visited her shop (and subsequently went through her accounts), it soon became apparent to me that she had not adjusted to the fact that the world outside her shop window had changed.

Instead of taking the necessary steps to ensure she attracted new business, she seemed content to wait for some magical turnaround or development that would bring customers flooding through her door again.

This was a situation made all the more frustrating by the fact that she was the nearest florist to the large Coombe Women & Infants University Hospital and several other potentially lucrative major clients such as local hotels, restaurants and the famous Guinness brewery.

Kim did have plans in place to help grow her business, by moving to bigger premises. But these were initially a source of concern to me. She brought us to a new retail unit she was looking at, which was a very big shop near the Coombe Hospital.

What appealed to her was that it was also beside a supermarket, and there would be greater passing traffic. This would be a good way of tackling the issue of declining footfall at her current location.

I felt that before even considering such a move Kim needed to first work at ensuring her business model was in tip-top shape. More specifically, she needed to conduct a root-and-branch review of her business.

Then, if she felt her core business was so strong that she needed to expand to have more space, such a move could make real business sense.

> While the temptation might be to batten down the hatches and remain in denial, it is vitally important to be able to react cleverly to external changes that impact on your business

But this was not the situation in which Kim found herself when we first visited her. If anything, it was the other way around: she did not have enough business to sustain her current premises, let alone a much larger one.

She needed to get this right first, before even contemplating such a significant expansion. Otherwise she would be doing things back to front, which is never a good thing in business!

One time I was preparing for a speech to the Irish Marketing Institute. I was speaking to a colleague of mine, and he said, 'The most important thing in business is location, location, location.' I recall nodding in agreement at the time.

But when I got home and thought about it a bit more, I realised I did not completely agree!

There's a saying from the nineteenth century that I have always liked: 'Build a better mousetrap, and the world will beat a path to your door.'

This has real merit in today's business climate.

Clearly, location is very important for some things. If I want a newspaper, and there's a newspaper shop on the left-hand side of the road as I am coming home, and there's one on the right-hand side across a busy road, then location is very important.

It's only a €1 purchase to buy the evening paper, so I am unlikely to cross the busy road to do it.

On the other hand, if I'm looking for flowers for a wedding, or going out for an important meal, I will go out of my way to find the right company, even if it's some distance away.

This was where I felt Kim should be pitching her business. She needed to build a better mousetrap.

This is all linked to the hugely important idea of becoming a destination, a theme we will discuss in more detail in Chapter 12.

It was clear to me that Kim's florist shop was going to succeed primarily because of her personality, her professionalism and the service she gave. Obviously, if there was busy passing traffic on the street this would make things even easier. But for now she needed to work with what she had rather than committing to an expensive relocation.

Many of her sales already came from the Internet, which, of course, is not dependent on location. And while her website was quite good, it needed to be even better, as there is huge scope to drive business through online floral retailing.

One of the major plus points with Kim is the fact that she has a great personality. She comes from a family that has been in the Liberties area of Dublin for generations.

She was very proud of her great-grandmother Biddy, to the extent that, without any prompting from me, she used her in all of the publicity we organised around the relaunch of the shop.

Kim was clearly great at using her heritage to her advantage. This was something I was chuffed to see. She built it up, and you could see a brand develop for Liberty Florist, firmly based on her heritage in the community.

She was also very keen to develop text marketing as a tool for her business. There are plenty of bad examples out there of businesses that get hold of your mobile phone number and bombard you with texts almost every day with their latest 'special offer'. That is not what text marketing is about. It should be about creating a 'club' that customers want to feel part of, as it gives them advance notice of exciting things happening at your business. And when they want to opt out, for whatever reason, every business should do their utmost to make sure this process is simple and hassle-free.

Kim spent months gathering phone numbers from customers who wanted to be on her database. Mother's Day was approaching, and she decided it was a good time to get in contact with these people.

On the Monday before Mother's Day she texted her customers this simple message: 'Kim here from Liberty Florist. Just to remind you next Sunday is Mother's Day.' The results were instant – and staggering!

Within minutes the phone started to ring, and web sales clicked away, as customers who were grateful for the reminder set about ensuring they marked the occasion with flowers from Liberty Florist.

By the time Mother's Day came and went, Kim had doubled her sales compared to the same week the previous year. This is customer service and marketing all rolled into one, in the most simple and effective way.

Yet despite Kim's warm and welcoming personality, and her wonderful willingness to develop new marketing and sales techniques, during the filming it became increasingly clear to me that something was holding her back.

Kim's confidence was not what it should have been; she was very nervous about making presentations to corporate clients. These types of clients can be a vital and very lucrative source of income for a small shop like Liberty Florist.

I knew this was something that we simply had to address. We brought her to bingo at the National Stadium in Dublin, where we told her she would have to get up on stage in front of hundreds of eager players and call out their numbers.

Suffice to say, Kim was more than a little bit nervous at the prospect and seriously doubted she could speak to so many people. In order to calm her nerves a bit, I told her I would go first.

I have to admit I am not exactly a novice when it comes to bingo-calling. During my youth at my father's holiday camp I was frequently asked to fulfil this very role.

But I hadn't called bingo for over forty years. And, as I stood staring down at the faces of these serious players, many of whom initially at least did not appear to appreciate the interruption, I was more than a little nervous myself!

Thankfully, within a matter of seconds it all came back to me, and before long I was calling out such phrases as 'two little ducks', 22, or 'two fat ladies', 88, as if I had never given up the job.

Next it was Kim's turn. At first, she was incredibly nervous, but she gained confidence very quickly, with the help of the crowd and its warm-up man.

To strike while the confidence iron was hot, shortly after the bingo we sent her to a well-known communications consultancy firm, where she learned about selling her wares to corporate clients.

Ultimately, she wowed the corporate people we had assembled as part of the show to listen to her pitch for their business.

Lisa Walsh, representing Jury's Inn Hotel in Christchurch (near to Liberty Florist), told us afterwards that the fact Kim was a supplier based in the local community was a key point for her company when it came to deciding whether or not to use her for their flowers.

Kim had of course been a member of the local business community for almost two decades but only now was anyone from Jury's Inn beginning to realise it.

Our work with Kim produced exciting results for her business. But this was only possible because of her total commitment to the cause: over the course of the show she fully acknowledged what she was doing wrong and worked darned hard to fix it.

More specifically, Kim knew that if she wanted her business to have any chance of surviving, she had to first change her patterns of behaviour. She had to come out from the darkness of denial and face the world, blinking in the sunlight.

And I am delighted to report that Kim recently opened her new, much larger, Liberty Florist shop. Importantly, the central location of the new premises means she has access to far more passing trade. Even more importantly for Kim, it is still located in the Liberties community where she has lived all of her life.

She explains that while trade in her old location was definitely up after she took part in the show, most of her orders were coming over the telephone or via the Internet. Although this was positive, Kim felt a larger shop that was less out of the way and that would allow her to properly display her goods would increase her business even further.

Clearly, Kim had things the right way around this time: it was only after she had taken the necessary steps to get her existing business on a more even keel that she took the considered decision to expand by relocating.

By getting the fundamentals of her business right first of all she could ultimately make the correct move for her, *for the right reasons.*

This is an approach that all struggling businesses would be well advised to adopt.

On a most basic level, when businesses like Kim's are faced with any 'shock' downturn scenario, they can do one of two things. They can carry on as before, remain in denial, and hope against hope that business will turn around for the better.

Unfortunately, the boarded-up corpses of many such retailers are to be seen in towns and villages around the country.

Alternatively, they can readily acknowledge the changed economic landscape in which they are operating and adapt accordingly, as Kim did, by focusing on what they need to do better and differently.

What's more, this can be a surprisingly enjoyable and ultimately rewarding process.

7

First impressions count

Learn to overcome your image problem

....

One of the first things I do when I walk into a shop is ask myself, what kind of message does this shop give me?

Do I feel welcome? Is it easy for me to find what I am looking for? Are the staff on hand to greet and guide me? Or do I feel intimidated, perhaps put off by the way the stock is presented, the layout of the shop, or the attitude of those working there?

Getting this first introduction to your customer right is absolutely crucial for any business. If you do it properly, then the chances are they will opt to give you their custom rather than give it to a rival further down the street, or even online.

....

But get it wrong and you risk not only alienating this customer but their many friends, family and work colleagues who will hear about the experience.

Green's Department Store is run by Florence Higgins and has been in the Higgins family for more than three generations. Covering over 550 square metres and located on the Ballyhaunis Road in Claremorris, Co. Mayo, it is a large country department store that offers a wide range including ladieswear, menswear, children's wear, babies wear, lingerie, clothes, haberdashery and homeware.

Florence is a capable businesswoman, who had already achieved a huge amount in her shop before we worked with her. Almost single-handedly she had managed to keep the shop ticking over during a difficult recession.

She was very open to new ideas, a vital trait in any successful business leader, and was not afraid to innovate. For example, seeing that she needed to increase her buying power, she had cleverly managed to forge a buying partnership with the much larger Shaw's retail chain, allowing her to have access to better stock at a more competitive price.

But, despite Florence's best efforts, times had never been tougher for Green's. Florence had really begun to feel the heat of the recession in recent months. On my first visit to the shop, it was at a crossroads, having suffered an 18 per cent drop in sales in the past year alone.

Clearly, more needed to be done if Florence was truly to turn things around.

Unfortunately for me, the first thing I saw when I

entered the shop was Bridget Jones-style 'granny knickers'. I like to think I am a relatively enlightened man, who has seen a lot during my career in business. But, I have to admit, the sight frightened me!

Their presence near the front of the shop risked discouraging other potential customers from exploring the shop. Like me, they might well have been put off by the sight of the underwear and the indirect first impression they were giving of the shop.

This is something that all businesses, and in particular small companies trying to fight for every piece of business during a recession, need to be very aware of.

They need to constantly ask themselves what it is like for a customer coming through their doors. More precisely, they should ask, 'What are the messages I am sending to someone as soon as they walk in to my shop, or look in my windows?'

What's more, they should ensure they listen to, and act upon, the answer.

It may seem pretty obvious that all businesses should aim to make a good first impression on their customers. Yet, during the *Feargal Quinn's Retail Therapy* series, I was genuinely shocked by how few of the businesses we visited managed to get this right.

All retailers should continuously strive to make life easy for their customers by having a simple logic to the way they present their stock. Rather than forcing customers to rummage around, they should make it as easy as possible for them to find, and ultimately purchase, what they are looking for.

One way we did this at Superquinn was by introducing a 'two-metre rule' in our shops.

I would regularly bring a two-metre-long stick with me as I visited our shops. And if I couldn't get through any part of the shop with this stick held horizontally, then the stock had to be moved.

Actually, I began using the stick after a customer in our Naas shop told me, 'My friend and I shop with you all year round, except at the busy weekends and coming up to Easter and Christmas.'

When I asked her why, she said, 'Well, you always make it so uncomfortable to shop with displays of Christmas crackers, or Easter Eggs, and you can't get around the place. We shop with you all year round, except at the busy times when we go somewhere else.'

The thinking behind my use of the stick was that there should be no aisle less than two metres wide. And I can assure you it was a thoroughly effective tool!

Over time, we worked alongside Florence to address the core image issues in her shop. She enthusiastically took part in a major review of the entire layout of the shop, which led her to move key departments closer to the customer as they entered.

At the same time, she greatly improved the lighting and the shop's front window to show how, sometimes, less can be more. Florence also developed the in-store merchandising and branding and created new points of interest for the shopper from a display perspective.

Despite the huge progress we made with Florence at Green's, I will say again: it continually astounds me just how many shops are failing to address their image problem.

For every Green's Department Store, there are potentially scores of others in a similar, or worse, situation.

So what is happening? Surely, during a time when consumer spending has been decimated, retailers are more aware than ever of the need to fight for every piece of business? Surely they are constantly looking to put their best foot forward?

I am sorry to report from the front line that, while there are of course some examples of excellence, there remain many more examples of poor layout and design.

It is as if some business people simply do not want to come out of the very comfortable, if increasingly tight-fitting rut into which they have squeezed themselves.

At this point, I have a confession to make: I do understand how this might happen.

Kind of!

Patterns of behaviour are frequently built up over the years, making it difficult for business owners to stand back and honestly assess just how far standards have slipped. Indeed, such slippage usually happens in small increments, over time, making it even harder to notice the overall change.

This is where the value of inviting a fresh pair of eyes into a business really comes into play.

> It continually astounds me just how many shops are failing to address their image problem

By allowing business owners or managers to see things through the eyes of an outsider, which is what all new customers essentially are, this can help to jolt them into action.

But in the absence of a sense of restless commitment to doing things better, many companies let their standards and their image slip.

Another example of how this can happen in even the most well established shops is Burgess Department Store.

The shop has a long and venerable history in the town of Athlone. At more than 170 years of age, it is Ireland's oldest department store.

It had a staff of forty-two when we visited, some of whom had been there since they left school over thirty years ago. It sold ladieswear, menswear, homeware and lingerie and also housed a couple of concession shops.

The town of Athlone changed hugely during the boom years, and the shop had to contend with the competition posed by the swish Athlone Towncentre, which housed high-street fashion chains from all over the world.

It was no surprise for me to hear that, like Green's, the shop had taken a huge hit when the recession began to really bite.

I spoke to Rosie Boles and her father Ian, who run the shop and who featured in my *Retail Therapy* series, about one of the most prominent signs in their shop.

Effectively, the sign advertised the shop as *the place* to be fitted for your bra in Athlone. This, of course, is excellent if you actually need to be fitted for a bra. But, just as with Green's 'granny knickers', it is a very limited selling point when you think of what an entire department store has to offer.

As a male, the sign also made me feel slightly uncomfortable and suggested this was not a place that really catered to men – or approximately half the population.

What was more, my concern was that it would probably not attract younger women to the shop's fashion offerings either.

But Burgess had bigger challenges than just tackling that bra-fitting sign. The sign turned out to be a symptom of a much wider problem facing the shop.

Burgess was primarily known amongst Athlone locals as a shop that catered for the older customer. Rosie gave us the example of a young man who saw a suit in the window that he liked but was too embarrassed to be seen in Burgess buying it.

One particular strength of the shop was its menswear section, where Ian, who is a born salesman, offered an excellent traditional gentlemen's outfitting service to customers.

Both Rosie and her father were doing their best to stay up to date with customer service and marketing trends.

However, since the recession hit, much of their efforts to keep the business going had so far focused on cutting costs. This was understandable, to a point. But there was a pressing need for a 'whole business' approach to tackling their serious image problem with a view to generating extra sales and getting new customers to come into (and remain loyal) to the shop.

Burgess needed to get the following message across to its customers, *'We are different to the chain stores. We have a uniqueness of offering. We are Irish. Make sure you check us out before you go to those big, generic multinational stores.'* Instead, it looked like things were being done pretty much the way they had always been done over the years. And this was helping to feed Burgess's image problem.

Burgess's definitely needed a lick of paint.

Windows are the start of the customer's journey. For any retailer, they represent one of the most important ways to capture the attention of the passer-by.

But, as with Green's, Burgess had too much stock in its windows – a common mistake.

Contrary to what some retailers believe, a sense of space inside a shop window can actually be more effective than a window crowded with stock as it is more relaxing to the eye. When people are relaxed they are more likely to enjoy what it is they are being offered.

Rosie's window was a real missed opportunity. It could have been the Brown Thomas or Selfridges shop window of Athlone. Instead, she had ended up with a boring, unimaginative display that was perhaps inadvertently aimed at older, and not particularly fashionable, women. Quite clearly, the outside of the shop and its prime location on Athlone's busiest street wasn't being max-imised.

In order to address this, we brought Rosie on a trip to London to see how one of the world's

leading department stores, Harvey Nichols, dresses its window displays. It is fair to say that Rosie was 'wowed' by their clearly laid out, uncluttered and attractive windows.

Crucially, she began to see how well-planned windows can be used not just to sell the goods on display but also to hint at what else might be inside the shop, encouraging customers to take a peep.

Once inside, Burgess also had work to do to make a positive impression on their customers.

When I first walked into the shop, the overwhelming feeling I had was of a tired, dated shop. This is very different to a well-established shop that portrays a confidence in itself and its heritage down through the generations.

More worryingly, it seemed not enough thought had been given to the directional signage and branding in the shop. Again, this is simply to show a customer how to get around the shop and to remind that customer, who may visit ten or fifteen shops that day, where it was they saw a particular bargain.

For example, when we walked into Burgess, we didn't even realise there was a cookery section downstairs or a household section.

Customers were not being coaxed to explore the shop. Again, this is an all-too-common failing among retailers.

Burgess needed to learn how to entice its clientele to check out its other departments by focusing on points of interest they would find attractive.

A sense of space inside a shop window can actually be more effective than a window crowded with stock

This can be done with advertisements highlighting special offers, details of newly added ranges and well-mounted displays of their wares.

As with Green's, Burgess needed to improve the layout of its stock in order to make it as easy as possible for customers to find their way around.

There was too much stock piled up high, leading to the sense of a cluttered shop floor. This did little to instil confidence in the customer.

It was also difficult to make out just how much stock Burgess actually had. There were little nooks and crannies everywhere.

I approached a young man on the street to ask him what he thought about the shop. He said that as a child he had been brought in to the boyswear section but that he would never have thought of going in there for his own clothes.

When he actually did go in, he could see that, yes, he would have shopped there had he realised that what they had was very good. In other words, the image of the shop was failing to correspond with its reality.

Rosie and Ian rightly identified the risk of throwing out the baby with the bathwater by alienating Burgess' existing customers in the chase for a younger clientele. This is something I hear time and again from retailers, particularly where shops feel they have a well-established customer base.

But, as with a newspaper whose circulation is under pressure, it is not enough to focus just on the customers (or readers) you have. You must also focus on the ones you wish to have. To do this, you need to have catchy headlines to lure them in.

There is always a reason why a shop is struggling; more often than not it is because it is giving neither its loyal customers nor its potential customers exactly what they want.

This is where social media such as Facebook and Twitter can be extraordinarily useful tools. It is no coincidence that some of the biggest retailers in the world now do a lot of their customer interaction and support through these types of social media.

Imagine being able to chat with thousands of customers in one day and to have them interact with your business whenever they feel like it? This is exactly what Facebook and Twitter allow you to do.

Recently an independent retailer showed me how they developed €10,000 of sales through Facebook by running a competition to generate interest in a new product they were stocking. In little more than three weeks, their Facebook profile had gained 15,000 new likes, as customers passed details of the competition from one to the other. This, of course, also meant that 15,000 new people saw the product. Many of them went on to buy it from the shop.

To her credit, Rosie was keenly aware of the potential

benefits of social media to her business. When we first went in to Burgess, she told me that she was setting aside time every day to update her Facebook page and to keep in touch with her customers. Impressed by her enthusiasm, we worked with her to extend her shop's social-media reach even further.

As part of the rebranding process for Burgess, we felt it was also very important for Rosie and Ian to consult extensively with staff and members of the public. Their feedback played a big role in deciding how the new shopfront and signage should look.

Other concrete steps we took at Burgess included an extensive decluttering and reorganising of the shop's retail area so that it was completely re-energised. This was coupled with the introduction of vastly improved signage to help direct customers, which went a long way to improving the overall customer experience.

Within a few short months, aided by Rosie and Ian's shared commitment to investing in their business, Burgess showed a new, more modern and confident face to the world. At the same time, it continued to serve its more traditional clientele.

The major measures they introduced at Burgess were simple, and for the most part inexpensive, changes that any business could introduce. As the old saying goes, where there is a will there is a way.

But the opposite is also true: without the will, there is just no way it will happen.

8

It's a listening thing

Don't make aliens of your customers

....

My friend Murray Raphel, the US marketing guru, tells a lovely story about a fourteen-year-old boy named Tommy who ran a gardening business. Murray, who as a retailer developed a major shopping mall in Atlantic City, New Jersey, had known Tommy since the day he was born and had delivered his baby clothes to his mother in hospital.

One afternoon, Murray was working in a store when Tommy came to the counter and asked him if he could use the phone. Murray heard him pick up the receiver and dial a number. A lady answered at the other end.

'Hi there, I just went past your house. Saw you had a

big lawn. I cut lawns to make some extra money. I also trim hedges. And I was wondering if …'

He paused, listened and then continued. 'I see. And are you satisfied with the work they are doing?'

Another pause.

'I see. Well, would it be all right if I called you back again in a month or so? I can? Thank you.' And he hung up.

Murray sensed his disappointment and walked over to the boy.

'Tommy, forgive me, but I was standing here and I heard everything you said. I want you to know that everything you said on the phone was great. Promise me you won't be disappointed because you didn't get the sale.'

Tommy answered, 'Oh, Mr Raphel, I got the sale. That was one of my customers. I was just checking up to see how I'm doing!'

I love that story because it encapsulates everything that is good about really valuing the customers you have. By (surreptitiously) checking in to see if his existing customer was happy with his service, Tommy was ensuring he could address any problems she might have had long before they became a potential deal-breaker for her.

This idea of truly valuing the customers you have is so very important for all businesses. Hence I find it puzzling to see how few businesses seem to agree with me.

Instead, they appear to prioritise attracting new customers rather than taking the time and effort to please the ones they already have. It is a huge personal gripe of mine.

I was sitting in my living room one day when Denise said a woman with an English accent had phoned for me. It transpired this was the second or third time she had phoned that week.

Each time, Denise had explained to her she was unlikely to catch me at home, and it would be better for her to try my office. But the mysterious woman just replied she would try me again at that number.

It is probably just as well my wife trusts me! As it happened, I was at home the next time the young woman rang. She told me she was from a well-known magazine and that my subscription was running out. She was calling me to ask if I would like to renew it.

'Actually, I enjoy the magazine, and I would like to continue my subscription. I would like to renew it. I'm delighted to see in the current edition that there's a 35 per cent reduction on it for subscribers,' I replied.

'Oh, no, that only applies to new customers!' she told me.

Now, I don't mind admitting that I went a little berserk when I heard this. I simply could not understand why someone who already had a subscription due for renewal was being treated with such apparent contempt.

But my young lady friend was not for turning. It was company policy, she informed me, and there was nothing she could do.

For this reason, I don't get the magazine any more. Instead, Denise, as a 'new' customer, subscribes to it for me.

The reason for my anger was simple: I felt the magazine company was quite blatantly saying it did not value my loyalty as much as that of a new subscriber.

To my mind, this is completely illogical. Rather than looking after someone who was already a paying customer, the magazine, in its wisdom, was prioritising complete strangers.

Unfortunately, it is an approach that is extremely common in modern business. Some of the very worst offenders are mobile-phone companies and other communications providers, whose advertisements frequently (and quite blatantly) state that their offers are only available to new customers.

The late Michael O'Connor, the former President of the American Supermarket Institute, had an excellent analogy that explains in a nutshell why it is so darned silly to ignore the loyalty of your existing customers. He described the marketplace as a leaky bathtub, with customers as the water.

When you are losing customers, it can be due to a variety of reasons: perhaps you are too dear, or your service or quality isn't good enough.

So what many companies do is try to turn on the tap above the bathtub, otherwise known as advertising. Because they are losing customers continuously, they spend huge amounts of their time and money getting new customers in to keep the bathtub up to a profitable level.

This is a very expensive way of doing things, as advertising is far from cheap. Wouldn't it be far better just to plug that hole by trying to find out what it is that is causing the leak in the first place?

If one of the leaks is because new customers are being offered better terms than existing customers, then I would argue that the company in question only has itself to blame. It should really be rewarding its loyal customers in the same way as it does its new customers by showing them it values their business equally. The beauty of such an approach, of course, is that it will also generate significant positive word of mouth, if it is handled correctly. This, once again, is exactly the type of advertising that no amount of marketing money can buy.

All businesses should try to introduce listening systems to allow them to stay close to their customers. This should be viewed as an important part of every employee's job.

Just like Murray's friend, it allows businesses to identify and fix potential problems at a very early stage. It also helps them to become truly customer-driven.

Indeed, businesses should never underestimate the impact that the simple act of *listening and reacting* to their customers' needs, no matter how big or small, can have in a competitive marketplace.

In my previous book, *Crowning the Customer*, I devoted an entire chapter to examining the types of separate listening channels that companies can use. All of the channels we used at Superquinn complemented one another, adding up to a rounded picture of what was really going on in the marketplace. The channels included:

- customer panels
- customer comment forms

- customer-service desks
- handling customer complaints positively
- inviting customer enquiries directly to staff
- managerial staff accessible to customers
- formal market research
- media comment.

In the book, I also noted the value of hostile or adverse comment, which should be reacted to constructively rather than defensively by any business. You can sometimes learn more from your critics than from your supporters.

There is another large group of people whose viewpoints can be hugely beneficial to any business that cares enough to listen to them. I would go so far as to say that you ignore them at your peril.

Who are these masked, mysterious people, I hear you ask?

Well, they are your non-customers, otherwise known as the people who have chosen not to frequent your business. At first glance, it may seem strange to seek the views of people who are not your customers. But it actually makes perfect sense.

The humble truth is, customers and non-customers know more than the management and staff of a business will ever know.

Why? Because it is they who make a conscious choice whether to spend their money with that business, or not, as the case may be. In other words, they are the only ones who do not have a vested interest in the business – unlike people whose jobs and livelihoods depend on the shop.

All businesses should try to introduce listening systems to allow them to stay close to their customers

Any business seeking to get a real handle on why it is not succeeding should actively seek out its non-customers too — be it by addressing the local community groups, charities, book clubs and other voluntary organisations — to find out what it is doing wrong.

It is no coincidence that one of the first things I did when I visited Green's in Claremorris was to listen to customers and non-customers of the shop, during a tea break at the town's largest employer, DeCare Dental Insurance.

What they told me, as is so often the case, helped hugely in our attempts to plot a way forward for the shop.

For example, one young lady told me that people like her go mainly to Castlebar, Co. Mayo, to shop for their clothes. This represented a real opportunity for Green's.

If Florence could offer a range of clothes to younger locals that allowed them to forgo this trip — or at least to consider checking out Green's first — then it would be a win-win situation for both the customer and for Green's.

Another woman at that meeting told me that she was not a customer of the shop. The reason she had not been there in years was because the last time she had been to the shop was as a child with her mother and she perceived it as being tailored towards older people.

'My mum would go there before me,' she said.

Interestingly, someone else said that if she heard there

You can sometimes learn more from your critics than from your supporters

was a new range in the shop, she would definitely take a look.

This was really throwing down the gauntlet to Green's: if it could improve its marketing and PR and add new stock, then people like these non-customers could potentially be converted into customers. This hugely valuable insight was not something a current customer of the shop was ever likely to tell us.

Another great example of the value of listening to your non-customers happened during our work with the Burgess Department Store in Athlone. Owner Rosie Boles was actually very good at listening to her customers. But it was unlikely she would hear the voices of those who would not be seen in her shop.

During the *Feargal Quinn's Retail Therapy* series, we established two customer panels: one featuring Burgess customers and another featuring non-customers. We put Rosie and her father Ian in a separate room with earphones so they could hear what their non-customers were saying.

As they sat there, they heard a number of home truths from the non-customers about their business, which customers would be too polite to point out.

For example, one young man relayed how if he wanted a suit he'd go to Dublin or to a rival shop across the road that had a nice window display rather than to Burgess. He never would have thought of going to Burgess for his suits. He was put off by the image of the shop.

Much of what Rosie and Ian heard that day made for difficult listening, and they did not agree with everything that was said. But listening to this adverse comment and turning it into constructive criticism helped them hugely in their efforts to analyse what Burgess was doing wrong. It provided real fuel for action, too.

All of us have probably had the experience of going into a restaurant or shop where the music is on for the staff rather than for the customer. Perhaps it is too loud or the music is too dance-oriented for the venue in question.

Of course this sends out completely the wrong message to potential customers: we will do what we want, and if you like it, great. If not, you know where you can go.

Despite our best intentions, sometimes we can send out similar messages to even our most loyal customers. Sometimes even when you think you are truly valuing your customers, the opposite can in fact be true.

Let me spell out just what I mean.

During the *Retail Therapy* series, Florence Higgins in Green's maintained that her employees greeted every customer. But when we tested this during our research for the television series, it transpired they tended only to greet the ones they knew.

In some respects this is completely understandable. People tend to say hello to the people with whom they have a relationship. Yet every business needs to be acutely aware of the very real risk of prioritising some customers at the expense of others in this way.

During one of our regular customer-feedback panels in Superquinn Blanchardstown, one customer told me, 'I love the butchers here, and Paddy is marvellous.' Her compliments were echoed by another woman, who added that 'Joe is marvellous too, he always looks after me, and he knows what I want. And he always gets me something special.'

But then a small, quiet woman in the corner piped up. 'Actually, I must get to know Paddy or Joe, or must get one of them to know me.' This struck me as a real concern. She clearly felt left out when she got 'What can I get for you, Madam?' Even though she shopped there all of the time, they didn't recognise her.

It was as if she simply did not count as much as some other customers, something that clearly left an unpleasant taste in her mouth. And in mine, too.

Not least because I knew exactly how she felt.

Almost twenty years ago, Denise and I ended up spending a week in the south of France, in a place called the Hotel du Cap-Eden-Roc, one of the most luxurious hotels in the area.

We had actually stayed there a few times before, but only for a day or two as it was so expensive. But having decided rather late to travel to the region, we booked into the five-star hotel, this time for six days.

It was an exceptional hotel in many ways, located in a beautiful part of France and with much to recommend it.

But, unfortunately, what I found really exceptional was that day after day after day I would go to the reception and nobody ever recognised me or ever called me by name.

What was more, every day I would also see the manager of the hotel fussing over other guests.

Now, we did not want to be fussed over, but we certainly felt left out as we watched the manager prioritising those guests whom he knew personally over us.

What is this saying to the paying customer whom your staff do not know? Are they less valued because of this? Do you risk making them feel alienated?

Are they aliens to you, when they should in fact be missionaries spreading the word about the brilliant work you do?

Nobody is saying that staff should know the name of every single customer in their shop. Of course, this would just not be feasible. But it is possible to chart a middle ground between welcoming those customers with whom your staff have a relationship whilst also showing other customers they are just as valued.

And the way to do this is very simple: make sure all customers are greeted warmly from the very moment they enter your shop to the time they leave.

Where possible, employees should also try to ask people for their names, too, even if they will not necessarily remember it down the line.

Unless the culture within an organisation is truly geared towards welcoming every customer, it can be very difficult to ensure no one slips through the net. While many companies pay lip service to the concept of greeting every customer, in my experience many fail to really embrace it.

This is where induction training comes in. If a company

says to its new employees on their first day that it is prioritising the greeting of all customers, this sends out a very powerful message: it tells new recruits that this is at the heart of the company's ethos.

Whenever I am in London, I make a point of staying in a relatively inexpensive hotel in Piccadilly.

The reason I do this is straightforward: every one of its customers is greeted by staff. And that is precisely why I love staying there!

When you get your key and walk along the corridor to your room, you invariably pass the cleaning people, most of whom do not have English as their first language.

Yet the staff there never pass me without greeting me. In my eyes, this immediately puts the hotel several levels ahead of any of its more expensive competitors.

I also suspect this is something that is addressed early on with staff during their induction training.

I encountered another excellent example of how to do this well when Denise and I visited South Carolina in the USA a few years ago. For years I had been encouraging our staff in Superquinn to introduce themselves and to call customers by name. But it was not in the Irish tradition, and many of our staff had difficulty doing it naturally.

Denise and I were staying in the Hilton Head Marriott Resort and Spa, and we were in Room 904, on the ninth floor. Now, this is a big hotel, and, as we had arrived there late, we decided to have dinner in our room. I phoned down to the restaurant, and a young female answered. She said,

'Good evening, restaurant here, Elaine speaking. What can I do for you, Mr Quinn?'

I gave our room-service order, which she took down diligently.

'By the way, where are you from?' she asked at the end.

'I'm from Ireland,' I answered.

'Sure, I know that! I'm from Ashbourne,' was the reply.

Elaine went on to tell me she was one of four Irish students who got J1 visas and were working at the hotel for the summer.

Of course, I know the telephone system gave the staff the name of who was ringing. But every time we phoned anywhere – the hotel golf shop, restaurant, reception, laundry, room service – they always called me by name, and they always introduced themselves. I thought this was just smashing.

We later went into one of the hotel's boutiques. The girl in the shop was busy serving a customer and did not notice us when we entered. But when she looked up and saw us there, she immediately apologised. 'I'm sorry, I never saw you come in, and I never greeted you.'

And her accent was thick with the Irish brogue too!

What excited me about this is that here were four nineteen- to twenty-year-old Irish people already doing this on their first two weeks in the job. They had only one hour's training. And yet they knew they had to adapt to the American way: greeting customers.

I don't think they would have automatically done that

at home, unless they had been told that this was something the company valued.

Whatever happens on the first day in any job is crucial. If you get into bad habits, these can be terribly hard to change.

An example of this was when we opened our Blackrock shop in 1984. Damien Kiernan was the shop manager charged with responsibility for about 200 staff.

When I went into the canteen with him for a cup of tea on his first day as manager, I said, 'Damien, look at the staff. They are not treating this as their own home; they are treating this as though it was a restaurant. Don't you know the company policy is to pick up your cup and saucer and put them back as you would in your own home when you finish your meal?'

And Damien said, 'I know, but they had developed the habit before I came here.'

Because the staff were working there already for some time we found it incredibly difficult to break this habit. In fact, we never got that right, and years later, although we tried as hard as we could, we still had to employ people in Blackrock to clear the tables.

This was not Damien's fault, as we had only appointed him to that shop a few weeks before it opened, meaning some of the staff had already begun their training before he arrived.

From then on, in all of our new shops, we appointed the shop manager a full nine months before the shop opened, so he or she set the tone for every single thing that was done in that shop.

You will not be surprised to hear that on the first day the staff came to work the manager told them that, 'the way we do things in this shop is as it is in your own home: you always take your cup and saucer and put them away yourself.'

And we have never had to hire someone to do this for our staff in any new Superquinn shop since.

One of my (secret) ambitions during my career in retailing was to have a system where every citizen had their Christian name printed on their forehead. Wouldn't that be smashing?

Actually, it would be anything but smashing, not least because even my competitors in business would use it.

But I hope you get my drift.

The famous US retailer Stew Leonard, who we will meet properly in Chapter 9, used to go even further. With every customer he saw coming in, he would imagine there was a $100,000 sign printed on their forehead.

He calculated that if he could convince each customer to spend $100 with him one week, and did such a good job that she kept choosing him over his competitors every week, then in the next fifty weeks she would spend $5,000.

Taking the long-term view, in twenty years she would spend $100,000 – a figure that suggested it was worth doing whatever it took to hold on to her.

One man who certainly knew the value of every customer was Bill Wilkins.

Bill was a very bright young man who joined us as an assistant manager in one of our bigger shops, Northside.

One day Bill expressed his frustration at seeing a customer with a trolley full of groceries being told she had to queue at a busy checkout as the express checkout was only for customers who bought a few items.

He went on to say he had once opened a shop of his own.

He took the shop over on a Saturday night, worked all day Sunday and opened it on the following Monday morning. At 8 a.m. he was ready for business and threw open his doors.

And nothing happened. He tidied up the shop a little bit more before he went outside and noticed the street his shop was on was rather empty.

Eventually, at around 9 a.m. – an hour after he opened – he saw a customer coming across the street ... but the man went next door.

At 9.10 a.m., a customer came in, and he met her with 'Hello, how are you? You are very welcome, what can I do for you?'

She said, 'I need change for the parking meter.'

At about half past nine, another customer came in and bought a bar of Cadbury's chocolate. She was so welcome at that stage that if she had bought a more expensive bar of chocolate, say a Toblerone, Bill told me he would have probably given her a lift home.

Bill lasted three weeks with his shop before he reluctantly pulled the shutters down. During those three weeks, the few customers who came in were treated royally by him. They were like a customer oasis in a retailing desert!

As Bill told me, 'You only have to go through what I did to value every single customer.'

This is something that has really stuck with me over the years. I found it very difficult to have any customer go past me without trying to make an impact on them in some way. Of course, what I was really trying to do was set a standard for everyone else at Superquinn to do the same.

One of the dangers of dealing with a lot of people is that you tend to think in mass terms and you don't think that every customer is a 'one-to-one' interaction. Yet every retailer has got to make every interaction with a customer just as important for them as it is for their customer.

Indeed, I have often thought if every business owner or manager, and their staff, could see the customer through Bill Wilkins' eyes, they wouldn't let a single one get away again without making some sort of an impact on them. This would mean that the customer would say, when given a choice between them and their competitors, 'I think I'll go back there even if it's out of my way.'

I believe everybody involved in a retail shop should wear a name badge in order to give their customer the opportunity to know their name.

When a company has a culture of greeting every customer, it is a source of real wonder to me. I am convinced there is a huge power in doing such a simple little thing. This was brought home to me again in our Blackrock shop just a few years ago.

> Every retailer has got to make every interaction with a customer just as important for them as it is for their customer

I was standing just inside the door when a customer came walking through. The Blackrock shop usually had around 25,000 people a week flowing through its doors. I was doing my best to catch people's eye and say, 'Hi', 'Hello', 'Welcome', 'Good to see you', 'How are you?', etc.

When this man came in, I greeted him, and he thanked me. About six or seven minutes later, he came over to me. He said, 'I have never been in such a friendly place in my life. I am not shopping, I happen to have a few minutes to spare, and I was in the centre so I came in.

'You greeted me as I walked in the door, but five or six other people caught my eye and greeted me as I went around the shop.' He continued, 'I never felt so good, so welcome! I was not actually buying anything; I had a few minutes to spare so I dropped in, but what a smashing place you have got here.'

What thrilled me about this was he wasn't talking about the excellent products and promotions we were offering in-store. Instead, he was talking about the welcoming attitude of our staff. They had made a true missionary out of him, and he would undoubtedly spread the good news to the rest of his social circle.

It really is amazing what a simple 'Céad míle fáilte' can do.

Sometimes in life you meet someone who is a master at what I call the 'Name Game'. And when you do, you seldom forget the experience.

Several years ago, Denise and I were at the CIES (the food business forum) grocery convention in the Concorde Lafayette Hotel in Paris. The event was on the twenty-sixth floor, the top floor.

Within the hotel, there is a special lift that only goes to the twenty-fifth and twenty-sixth floors.

As it happened, the French Open tennis tournament was on that week, and the Concorde Lafayette was where many of those involved with the tournament were staying. As you can imagine, it was very busy, with loads of activity.

We stepped into the lift, and just as the doors were closing an attractive woman came in carrying her tennis gear. She was obviously a tennis player.

Now, I have never been one to observe an awkward silence, so I asked her politely, 'Were you playing today?'

'Yes, I was!' she replied.

'How did you do?'

'Oh, I won today.'

'And who were you playing against?'

'Oh, against the Italian player.'

I asked, 'Do you mind telling me your name?'

She said, 'I'm Mary Joe Fernández.'

Mary Joe was a very famous tennis player at the time, who hailed from Florida.

I said, 'Mary Joe, I'm sorry, I should have recognised you! I didn't recognise you, I'm so sorry.'

We came to the twenty-fifth floor, and I said again, 'Mary Joe, I'm sorry, I should have recognised you. My apologies.'

As she was leaving the lift, she turned around and said, 'You're Feargal Quinn, aren't you?'

With that, the door closed, and she was gone.

I turned to Denise, flabbergasted.

'Denise, I have no idea how she knows my name ... I've never met her before!'

I turned an even brighter shade of purple when Denise calmly pointed to the name badge on my lapel, which Mary Joe had obviously clocked as soon as she entered the lift.

9

Make heroes of your staff

Delegate, delegate, delegate

....

Throughout my time with Superquinn, I operated off a pretty simple premise: my employees will continually surprise me if I empower them sufficiently to exceed my expectations.

Some years ago, I challenged several of my colleagues to define what management was, in five words or fewer. During our discussions, we threw numerous ideas back and forth.

It is a surprisingly difficult word to capture, as management encompasses so many different aspects of working life, including HR (or, as I much prefer, the talent department), recruitment, finance, purchasing, marketing, sales and public relations.

Eventually, after extensive debate, we settled on, 'Getting results through other people.' Without wishing to blow our own trumpets, I have always thought this an excellent working definition of the term. Why?

Well, because one key way of getting other people to deliver results is by delegating responsibility.

It is a straightforward concept. If a business is going to succeed, then surely it is the people who work there who will make this happen.

Yet it surprises me how rarely this occurs, even in some very large, successful organisations. Frequently, the fear of being ruled by diktat from a large company's HQ can actually serve to inhibit the creative abilities of its employees.

This is where small businesses in particular can hold a trump card in a recession: remaining close not just to their customers but also to their employees, making it much easier to show them just how much they trust their initiative.

By demonstrating to your staff publicly that you believe in them, the faith you place will often be rewarded in spadefuls.

One way of encouraging your employees to take pride in what they do could hardly be simpler: calling them by name and letting your customers know them by name.

You can imagine my frustration when I found that, even in some of the bigger shops we visited during *Feargal Quinn's Retail Therapy*, employee name badges were almost completely absent. Such badges are hugely useful for customers who feel better when they can say 'Hi Catherine' or 'Hello

John' to the person there to serve them, particularly if they have dealt with them before.

What's more, it also allows the person working there to have a sense of ownership over what it is they are doing. They are not just a faceless worker in the shop but a real human being with whom the customers can interact.

This sense of ownership can be extended further.

For example, Jane Smith is sixteen, and she starts off sweeping the floor. Then, with time, she progresses to another section of the shop, before being put in charge of a section with two others working under her.

If you take Jane's photograph and put it over her section, you are honouring her work and the progress she has made to date. When you let the world know that 'Jane Smith is now in charge of the tinned beans section', that is in itself hugely empowering.

It is also making a hero of her.

This is because her mother, her neighbours, her aunt and her former school pals who come into the shop for their weekly shopping will see it and say, 'Ah, she is actually in charge of a section now. Isn't it great to see her doing so well?'

There is little doubt that a sense of being trusted and put in charge, coupled with the social proof of your neighbours and friends seeing this can really help empower and energise your employees.

This can be extended to including photos of your employees in promotional material for your shops, which is something we regularly did at Superquinn.

One year, at the start of our big year-end management meeting, we went a step further.

We took a photograph of every shop and of the shop manager. Then we superimposed the manager's name in place of the word 'Superquinn' over the door of the shop. In the large framed photograph, the shop became 'James Burke's', 'Keith Harford's', 'Cormac Tobin's', etc.

The reason we did this was to show our managers that we wanted them to run their shop as though it was their own.

Of course we made sure to give them plenty of hints, suggestions and back-up support – everything we felt they needed to succeed.

Behind all this was the idea that ultimately we saw the shop as their baby, to develop in a way they were happy with.

Truly making heroes of your staff means allowing them to show their own initiative and judgement, no matter their job title within the company.

In management speak it has become known as 'empowerment', but in Superquinn we have for years simply called it 'Making Everyone a Manager'.

And here is how it worked in practice for us.

One day, Ray Clarke, manager of the newly opened Superquinn Lucan, showed me a letter he had just received.

It was from a customer who had visited the supermarket for the first time earlier in the week. This customer recalled how he had said to the checkout operator, 'We think we have spent more than we have. We have only £60, would you ever stop the bill at £60?'

The bill came to £78, and he threw his eyes to Heaven when the checkout operator told him this. He was very embarrassed that she had not followed his wishes.

Then she said something that really surprised him. 'Now, my name is Marie. I'm at checkout no. 8. When you come back with the £18, give it to me because my cash won't balance.'

He was astounded at this response. 'Are you trusting me with £18, even though it is my first time ever being in the shop?'

'Yes,' was her reply.

His second question was, 'But you are just a checkout operator, have you even got the authority to do that?'

To which she replied, 'Yes. The manager said we can make that decision. Now, I wouldn't trust everyone, but I do trust you.'

The letter Ray showed me that day had been handed in with the £18 from the customer, who was overwhelmed with gratitude.

I have to admit I was a bit taken aback myself that a checkout operator could make such a potentially costly decision. 'Ray, do you really let the checkout operators decide?' I asked.

'Yes,' he replied. 'There are so many people who were succumbing to our tasty food that they were spending more than they had with them! Invariably I was getting a call every five minutes to say there was someone at the checkout who needed to be allowed credit. I gathered all of the checkout operators around me and told them, "You make the decision in future."

'Since then, nobody has let me down. And I think it is because the customers feel they don't owe the money to the big supermarket but to Marie on checkout no. 8.'

By far the best example I know of somebody who knew the importance of making heroes of his employees is Stew Leonard. Stew is a legend among retailers. He started with one food store in Norwalk, Connecticut, and now has four.

On the walls in all of his shops are little paper ladders showing where each of the store's employees started out. More importantly, it shows where they are now in the store's management chain.

Using the fictional example of Jane Smith from earlier, Jane would be introduced as having started as a floor sweeper. Her next step was to tinned beans, and then perhaps to the checkout, before returning to manage the tinned-vegetables section.

This paper ladder, which employees and customers alike can see, very effectively validates the contribution that every member of staff makes to the success of the shop.

You are automatically linking their history to the development of the shop. And, by so doing, you are very publicly empowering the people who work for you. You are showing them you are proud of them, and you are showing their contacts that they are valued by you.

Another good way to ensure your employees remain motivated is by making work fun.

A small business owner struggling with finances might wonder how on earth they can afford to make work fun, when it is all they can do to keep the doors of their shop open.

But I would argue that there are many simple, relatively inexpensive ways of doing so, once you are committed to thinking outside of the box. Again, just as we saw with fun customer competitions in a previous chapter, this is where suppliers can play a role.

For example, you could ask one of your suppliers to reward the employee who manages to sell the largest amount of their product over a certain period of time. The reward could be relatively small – a gift voucher or a hamper, for example.

Alternatively, you could run a competition to come up with the most novel marketing or PR idea for the shop and ask your employees to take part. Again, the reward could be sponsored by a supplier or other local business, perhaps by way of a reciprocal arrangement with their employees. Or you might give the winner an extra day off work.

By introducing a sense of novelty to your business you are creating a sense of excitement and competition for your employees. The enthusiasm you will receive in return is invariably well worth the effort.

Another way of making a hero of your employees is by showing each one that you see them not just as a faceless employee but as an individual with family, friends and a unique personal story.

This has to do partly with being the employer of first choice in a competitive marketplace. Again, it is about setting the tone for your company, this time by demonstrating to your colleagues just what they mean to you.

At Superquinn, we endeavoured to do this in a variety of ways. Some of these were simple, like offering access to free medical care for all employees or organising competitions with prizes of study trips abroad.

But, as with our approach to our business, we continually sought to go further than this, in order to show our staff how much we appreciated the work they did on our behalf.

For example, each year in the run-up to Christmas, we recognised everyone who was celebrating their fifth (tenth and later fifteenth, etc.) anniversaries with the company that year by holding a dinner and dance at a posh hotel in Dublin.

All those present had their photograph taken with their spouse, Denise and me. This photograph was then presented to them, framed, at the end of the evening.

We could have just marked these occasions with a simple watch, or gift certificate – if indeed we wanted to mark them at all. It would have been a lot easier too.

But instead we felt it was important to make a social event of this landmark occasion. By so doing, we wanted to show how much we valued our colleagues' loyalty.

The purpose was to make our employees feel that, irrespective of their role within the company, they were part of a workplace community rather than just being anonymous workers in some supermarket chain.

This was something we further reinforced by very often including photos of our staff in our Superquinn advertisements as a way of celebrating their contribution to our company.

Also, I signed a card to every member of staff at Christmas, as another small token of my appreciation. Where possible, I would try to include a personal message – for example, if they had given birth to a child that year or had lost a relative or loved one.

As you can imagine, this was a huge logistical exercise, given the thousands of people Superquinn eventually employed. As the company grew, I found I had to start the process earlier and earlier so that towards the end of my time at the helm of the company I started signing these Christmas cards in October!

We also encouraged our people to study. If any employee enrolled on a course that was useful to their job, we would give them study leave and time off for exams, and we would reimburse them upon successful completion. This applied even if the course had only an indirect link to their role at Superquinn. For example, we paid for people to learn French or sign language (which actually turned out to be hugely useful in our shops).

Our one requirement was that everyone who signed up to a course, and had our approval to do it, went on to finish it.

The biggest annual event of all at Superquinn was St Patrick's Day. Every year we announced we were going to put a group into the St Patrick's Day Parade, and anybody who wanted to take part was welcome. Those who signed up volunteered to give their free time to practise each Sunday for four weeks ahead of the day. About 400 staff would take part, and they would almost fight to get involved with it. It was great craic!

We had dancing and singing on our parade floats, and everyone had to come all dressed up in their best uniform. On the day itself, we met for breakfast and then headed in to St Stephen's Green at the crack of dawn. On our last year taking part the theme was 'Simply the Best!' and we had our routines rehearsed well.

Each year we had three floats and we cooked 40,000 sausages on them. Twelve of us dressed as butchers, and we ran and ran the whole length of the parade. I was always one of the twelve butchers, shouting 'Have a hot Superquinn sausage!' People would clamour for them behind the barriers.

I recall only one time when my sausage was refused, and that was when I found myself staring into the eyes of Ireland's Chief Rabbi, David Rosen, who happened to be a friend of mine. Understandably, he was not a pork-sausage enthusiast!

After the parade, we had food and a disco in Dublin's Gresham Hotel for our parade team as a thank you. This was all about making a real virtue of our workplace as a community and showing our colleagues they were the real heroes of the company.

Looking back, I think one of the reasons Superquinn was the best place to shop was because you were welcomed in, you were looked after and you got friendly service. But to get friendly service you really had to have people who enjoyed working there, who felt part of something bigger.

This was brought home to me when a colleague, John Davitt, came to me in mid-December 1993 to say, 'Feargal, I am going to be sixty-five on 31 December. I know you would like me to continue to work for a few hours each week, if only to train the newcomers in. But my wife and I, there are things we want to do, and we have agreed that I am going to stop work.

'I just want to say I have worked here for nine years. I have had other jobs for the previous thirty years of my life but I have worked here for nine years, and I haven't missed a day. I wake up in the morning looking forward to coming to work. It's been great. I love working here. I look at my watch in the afternoon thinking it must be about 4 p.m. and it turns out to be 6 p.m. The day has gone faster than I thought.'

John died on Christmas Day that year, six days before he was due to retire. His wife died three days later. We had two very sad funerals in Ballinteer that same week. And we talked about John a lot afterwards.

We asked ourselves, 'How can we ensure that all our staff would say, as John Davitt did, "I wake up in the morning looking forward to coming to work. I look at my watch at 4 p.m. And discover it is 6 p.m.?"'

We couldn't pay more than our competitors; we couldn't give longer holidays, or longer tea breaks. But we could find other ways — such as allowing them to use their own flair and initiative in their jobs, or encouraging them to enjoy the fun of the St Patrick's Day parade — to ensure we let our staff know just what they meant to us.

We also wanted to always have the choice of the very best people. If there was a job going at Superquinn or elsewhere, ours was the company people wanted to work in most of all.

I was reminded of the importance of making heroes of your staff when we visited Sampson's Butchers in Drogheda for the final programme of the second series of *Retail Therapy*. We saw a shop facing a major battle to survive in a very competitive marketplace.

This traditional butchery shop had been set up by Eamonn Sampson in 1960 and had successfully traded as a going concern in the town for fifty years. Eamonn, who sadly passed away during the filming of the programme, had handed over the reins to his son John a few years earlier.

But now the shop was struggling to attract new customers and to move with the times. Sampson's desperately needed to move into the twenty-first century, without compromising on its traditional charm and 'farm to fork' philosophy.

Although it was a small business with only a handful of employees, we soon realised that it had a secret weapon. While there, I had been thoroughly impressed by Gerry and Kevin who worked alongside John in this small butcher's shop.

One of my chief concerns with Sampson's was the type of products it was offering. At a time when customers are increasingly looking for high-quality, good-value, ready-to-cook meals, John's shop was stuck in the old way of doing things.

His products were good value and excellent quality, and were sourced from his own farm, so customers could trace them back to their point of origin. But they were not oven-ready or being prepared for the demands of today's market-place.

Unfortunately for John, this was in stark contrast to many of his competitors, so his customers were flocking elsewhere.

John was not doing enough to brand his shop either. He confided at one stage that he had a sign up telling custom-ers where his meat came from. This should have been a very positive selling point for his business. You can imagine my dismay when he added that it was not prominently displayed as he did not want to 'push it down their throats'!

He should have been shouting from the rooftops that customers should shop with him because he was different, unique, and the beef came from his own farm. Instead, he was simply relying on the same tried-and-tested formula that may have been relevant forty or fifty years ago but would not cut the mustard in today's marketplace.

John needed to instil confidence in his customers, too.

His window display emphasised that he sold cheap meat, whereas I felt it should be emphasising the quality and value of his offering – a very different type of emphasis indeed.

I asked Pat Whelan, from the award-winning James Whelan's butchers in Clonmel, Co. Tipperary, to come to Drogheda to take stock of what was going on in John's shop.

As Pat put it, the food John was offering was in its primary state. He felt it needed to be sold in a far more kitchen-ready state, and John witnessed at first hand how to do this when he visited Pat's own shop. During the visit, Pat explained the aim of preparing products in this way was to get people excited about the taste, quality and flavour of the food.

I could see that John was not initially enthused about the proposed changes to his business. He told me that he felt it important 'not to throw the baby out with the bathwater'.

My belief was if he did not react quickly and decisively the baby would have no bathwater at all.

Unfortunately, as is so often the case with small businesses, Sampson's was stuck in the old ways of doing things. It was standing still and losing trade rather than moving forward and developing its business.

It had failed to keep up with a key new trend in meat retailing, namely ready-to-cook food that customers could just pop into the oven or onto the frying pan when they got home from work.

By comparison, when John visited Pat's butchers, he could see how Pat and his team were trading on the basis of a long-term sustainable relationship with their customers.

They did this by offering premium food, at a good price, coupled with signage that communicated this message to the customer.

While things were looking pretty bleak for Sampson's, there were positives in the shop too.

Gerry had impressed me with his enthusiasm. Seeing his energy and 'can-do' attitude gave me renewed confidence that this could be harnessed for the good of the shop.

If Sampson's was going to succeed, John needed to realise the importance of delegating tasks to Gerry so that his talents could be used to full effect.

I told him as much, in one of our on-camera interviews. 'I've learned that in my business there are certain things I couldn't do as well as others. Same with you, John, you can't do it all on your own,' I suggested.

I was absolutely delighted, and impressed, with the response I received.

'You have to delegate,' he agreed.

My hope was that the delegation penny was beginning to drop. And it was not long before John put his commitment to delegation into action.

As our time together progressed, and we prepared for the relaunch of the shop, he happily relied on Gerry to come up with a window display showcasing Sampson's new range of ready-to-cook foods.

By the time the doors to the shop reopened, following its extensive revamp, it was like a completely new shop. One customer even told us that it 'stops you in your tracks' — which of course was music to our ears.

I have been back to visit Sampson's on several occasions since the show first aired. In the past when I went there, Gerry would typically have been behind the counter, working away trying to keep busy. He had little else to do!

But when we walked in recently, I was delighted to see John in his uniform, full of energy and resplendent in his straw boater. Standing nearby was his lieutenant Gerry, who was positively bubbling with energy and enthusiasm from behind the counter.

The meat counter was packed, and there were many customers. The shop had also taken on an extra employee, increasing their staff from three to four. This is no mean feat in a recession.

The ready-to-cook food was displayed prominently, and the whole shop looked modern, fresh and hygienic. Meanwhile, the branding within the shop was excellent, highlighting a whole range of new products.

Gerry had been made a hero by his boss, John, through his participation in the programme. And the results were simply wonderful for all to see.

The lesson in all of this is it is important to stay close not just to your customers but to your employees too. They are, after all, the engine that will drive the success of your business — all the more so when times are difficult. You do this by making heroes of them and trusting their instincts by showing them you are willing to delegate. In my experience, if you allow yourself to be surprised by your employees, it will be repaid tenfold when they go further than you may ever have thought possible.

I have always been impressed at the talent people have when it is unleashed and allowed to breathe.

But in order to really do this, I believe it is just as crucial that any successful company allows its employees to take risks, within reason. It is only through trying something out that you will learn what will, and will not, work for your customers.

This is about trusting your employees enough to let them fail, something we will look at in more detail in the next chapter.

10

Take risks

Why failure should always be an option in your business

....

We saw in Chapter 5 how Caroline at Carrie's Cakes had been willing to take the risk of incurring more debt in order to secure the future of her business. She did this only after carefully considering the pros and cons of such a move, before bravely sanctioning the investment she needed.

In Chapter 9, we saw how John in Sampson's Butchers learned to delegate to his right-hand man Gerry. By placing his trust in him, he was repaid in spadefuls by an enthusiastic employee, eager to show his faith was justified.

One of the best ways a boss can demonstrate his or her

....

trust in an employee, and ultimately their own business, is by allowing them to take risks. Even more importantly, no one in your business should be afraid to fail.

What can I possibly mean? Surely it is never a good idea to create a risk-taking culture within your company that could lead to potentially costly failures?

Well, while it pains me a little to admit it, when I look back at my career in retailing I can all-too-readily remember the times when we blundered. But, far from regretting this, I would not have had it any other way.

One such instance relates to the time we considered introducing live fish into our shops.

As part of our ongoing attempts to keep abreast of developments in the marketplace, I frequently travelled around the world looking at the different innovations in supermarkets. Such trips were an important source of new ideas.

One time, in Japan, I saw that customers wouldn't buy fish unless they were alive at the time of purchase. During a routine business trip to Atlanta, Georgia, I witnessed something similar in the city's famous Dekalb Farmers Market. The fish on sale was all alive at the time of purchase.

The way it worked was you bought your fish by pointing out the one you wanted. The fishmonger took it out, put it on a slab with your name and your receipt on it.

When you came back ten or fifteen minutes later, you collected the fish you had chosen, and it had been cleaned for you.

Buoyed by what I had seen in Japan and Atlanta, I decided this was the best idea ever! By allowing a customer to choose the exact fish they wanted, I felt we could give our customers a real sense that they were personally in charge of selecting their purchase. Rather than some anonymous fishmonger selecting their food for them, they would be empowered to make this decision for themselves.

Armed with my big idea, we introduced live fish in our Blackrock shop, on a trial basis. Once the trial was up and running, we sat back and waited for the customers to respond with the same enthusiasm we had for the innovation.

It was a complete and utter failure.

And it soon became clear to us why.

We had failed to realise that the Irish market is very different to the Asian one. While the process of picking out your fish alive is culturally acceptable in Asia, or in countries with a strong Asian population, such as the USA, in Ireland people just did not want to see their dinner alive shortly before they brought it home to eat.

In our enthusiasm for our new idea, we had neglected to consider whether Irish people would actually stomach such an innovation. It turned out they would not; therefore, our great plan to revolutionise the fishmonger business in our supermarkets came to nothing.

We had a similar experience when we tried to introduce live lobsters in our shops. We had thought, because you frequently saw live lobsters for sale in upmarket restaurants here, that Irish customers might have become accustomed to the practice of choosing their lobster.

We could not have been more wrong. Far from loving the idea of picking out their lobster fresh from the super-market, many of our customers recoiled at the thought, feeling it was just too cruel. It clearly upset many custom-ers, so again we had to take it away.

Another glorious failure for Superquinn was our idea to sell food in bulk. Back when I was Chairman of An Post I was in Canada on a business trip. I was hungry after travelling all day, so I sat down to get a sandwich.

While waiting for my food to arrive, I happened to pick up a newspaper and saw huge ads for bulk food. These offered many of the same goods you would see on the shelves, at heavily discounted prices.

I was so excited with the concept that I asked the hotel porter where the nearest store was. Off I went, straight away, leaving my sandwich behind me. I jumped into a taxi, and the taxi driver told me that Loblaw's did the best bulk food. It was where his wife always shopped, and he thought bulk food was just wonderful.

The way the bulk-food system worked was you would have barrels or other big containers of dry goods such as cereals, soup mix, rice, etc., and customers would fill a plastic bag with the amount they wanted. These would be weighed and then taken to the checkout.

Because the retailer was saving on packaging, brand-ing and other costs, this allowed them to offer the goods at a very significant discount. And, as I saw in that Loblaw's store, sales were certainly booming!

When I came back to Dublin I was so excited by the concept that four of our people flew to Toronto specifically to see how it worked in Loblaw's. They returned equally enthused, so we set about launching the concept in our shops. This was in 1983, and my colleague Damien Carolan oversaw its implementation.

We thought it was a great idea as we were able to reduce prices significantly. For example, the soup mix in the bin was typically one-fifth of the price of Erin Food's soup. We placed large bins with scoops in all of our shops and pushed our bulk-product initiative with our customers.

But again there was a fatal flaw in our great plans: it was perceived as unhygienic by our customers.

This was brought home to us one evening when we saw a man licking his fingers and tasting each of the products on sale. We beat a hasty retreat from the idea, as this was definitely not an image we wanted to put across in our shops!

And then there was Tusa Bank.

We went to Richmond, Virginia, to visit a great supermarket company called Ukrop's some years ago. Ukrop's was about the same size as Superquinn, and, like us, it was a high-quality family business, centred around a clearly defined geographical area, with a strong emphasis on fresh food coupled with the personal touch.

While they did some things differently to Superquinn (for example, they had one central bakery whereas we had a bakery in each shop), in many ways they were very similar to us as a business.

Over the years, we got to know them well. We travelled to Richmond quite frequently, and they reciprocated by coming to visit us in Dublin. I always thoroughly enjoyed the exchange of ideas that such visits permitted.

Jim Ukrop, who ran the company, came to me one day and said, 'I want to interest you in a new business we've got involved in.' I listened intently as he explained.

'We have tied up with a bank, and we are putting our own bank into each shop. We will own 50 per cent of the new bank. It is hugely successful to the extent that I am going to become chairman of the bank. I'm going to step out from the grocery end and hand that to my brother Bobby.'

His family company would still own and run the Ukrop's stores, but I knew this was a very significant decision for a man like Jim to make. The success of his business had always been centred around Ukrop's knowledge of the supermarket trade.

Yet here he was, willing to move away to focus instead on a completely new area: banking.

I was aware that this was not a decision he would have taken lightly and was struck by just how much potential he must have seen in the new venture. Intrigued, I sent our financial director, Frank Murphy, to Richmond to take a look. He came back very enthusiastic.

Frank felt, as did I, that we had a real opportunity to introduce the first supermarket-based banks into the Irish market. We brought the Trustee Savings Bank (TSB) on board to help us and decided to go ahead with a similar project in our Superquinn shops.

On 20 October 1999, Tusa, the first supermarket in-store banking service in Europe, opened for business in Superquinn Lucan. Tusa is the Irish for 'you', 'yourself'. Operating as an agent of TSB, it provided a full range of personal-banking services including current accounts, credit-card facilities, personal loans, mortgages and saving plans.

The initial investment in the venture was over £5 million. By tying up with TSB, we were eventually able to open a chain of fourteen branches in the Superquinn supermarkets. We took on as many as 100 people and waited for the success that Jim Ukrop had experienced in Richmond to be replicated in our shops.

There was one snag. While we had all of the correct infrastructure and staff in place, we soon discovered we were doing virtually no business! Unsurprisingly, we weren't making a profit, either.

The fatal flaw in our plans? Well, in the USA, people coming in to do their shopping would go to the bank and open an account or apply for a loan. Before they got to the checkout, the loan would be approved. That's the way they do things in the States (or at least that was the way they did things until the banking sector collapsed there).

But due to strict Irish laws against money laundering, and other reasons, the Tusa staff had so much paperwork to get through that it was impossible to open accounts as quickly as they did in Richmond.

The requirement in Ireland was for people to have their passports with them in-store, as well as a record of where they had banked before. This made the whole process far more cumbersome than in the USA. It also meant that the attraction of being able to apply for a loan while doing your weekly shop was not there.

Put simply, our Tusa bank was not a convenient way of doing business.

Eventually, we had to pull the plug on the Tusa experiment, but not before incurring significant losses. Clearly we had misjudged the ability to transfer something from one jurisdiction to another. And this meant that Tusa Bank was a failure.

While this hit us financially in a big way, it was even more difficult to have to tell the loyal Tusa staff that there was no longer any job for them. This was the most difficult job that I ever had to do in Superquinn. A number of the Tusa team had left good jobs with banks to join us, and I felt I had let them down.

Ukrop's bank, however, continues to thrive to this day.

There are many more instances of my staff and me taking risks that ended in failure for Superquinn.

To give another example, Kieron Ellis, our manager in Walkinstown, was an avid consumer of Chinese food. On a trip to the USA, he came upon a wok kitchen in a supermarket and returned home full of enthusiasm to start a Superquinn wok kitchen, which would allow people to buy freshly made Chinese food. We let him trial it in-store, although we soon realised there was not enough demand among our customer base for this particular innovation.

Another time, my colleague Brendan Cryan was in a Metro store in Germany and saw staff members on skates. We thought it would be a great idea for our bigger shops. We put a sign on the checkout saying, 'Forgotten something? Let us get it for you. It won't take long as we have skates.'

But the idea did not really take hold, not least because the insurance companies were aghast at the concept, and eventually we abandoned it. However, I recently saw it in operation in Carrefour in France.

There is a reason why I am taking the time to high-light (in excruciatingly painful detail) the above failures so openly. Trust me, it would be far easier for me to only acknowledge our successes. Nobody likes being reminded of their failures.

When things did not work out in Superquinn, we always made sure to examine the reasons for these failures care-fully. This was only prudent if we were to avoid making the same mistakes again. I am proud to say that nobody got a slap on their wrist in Superquinn if they failed.

Instead, the culture of the company meant they were told to go away and come back with another idea that would work the next time around. There was an attitude within the company that accepted that mistakes do happen. More importantly, the message we gave our staff was that the risk of failure should never be used as an excuse not to try.

The reason for this?

Well, first of all it encouraged innovative thinking amongst our staff, something that is vital for all businesses, particularly during a recession. This also allows ambitious staff to show just what they can do, without fear of retribution.

If a member of staff can see a colleague's idea being implemented in the company, this creates a real motivation for them to follow suit by coming up with good ideas of their own.

One day, Ray Connolly, who was in charge of the fruit counter in Superquinn Ballinteer, said to me, 'Feargal, have a look at the kumquats.'

He explained that he had put a young guy named Shane in charge of the exotic-fruit department. He had been more than a little taken aback when Shane came to him a week later and said, 'Ray, I think we should do away with the exotic-fruit department.

'I watched last week, and very few customers came in with exotic fruit on their list. Instead of making it an exotic-fruit department, let's do the exotic fruit in little cake baskets.'

So, Shane got baskets from the cake department. He put the kumquats and other exotic fruit in them, before placing these fruits in front of the bananas, apples, oranges and other more common fruits. Then, when people came along to the orange section, they found mangoes in front of the oranges, and when they came along to buy apples they found the kumquats in front of the apples.

This had the effect of enticing people who hadn't come
with kumquats and mangoes on
their shopping list to consider buying them.

The risk of failure should never be used as an excuse not to try

And it worked a treat. Where Ray used to sell only one box of kumquats a month he started to sell one a week.

Shane's colleagues in our other shops heard about what he had done. A week later, I was in our Sundrive shop, and the supervisor, John, said to me, 'Have a look at what Karina has done.'

Karina said, 'I've copied what Shane did in Ballinteer, and I've put the exotic fruits in front of the apples. People see them better now. But the other thing is I got an encyclopedia of gardening and cut out the entry on kumquats. You know, where they come from, recipes for them, what to do with them, and I covered it in a little bit of plastic. And now people know about kumquats. Since we changed the way we displayed the kumquats, I'm selling two boxes a week instead of one box a week.'

Karina was only sixteen or seventeen years old, but she clearly was being allowed to use her initiative in a very positive way.

A few days later, I was in Superquinn Bray, and Andrew, the manager there, said to me, 'Have a look at what Ronan is doing with the kumquats.'

Ronan told me he used to sell one box a month, then one box a week, and now two boxes a week as he had copied Shane and Karina too. Then he added, 'But last week we sold four boxes of kumquats alone.'

'What did you do?' I asked.

He said, 'All I did was change the price from weight to per unit. Instead of selling them at X amount per kilo, I sold them at 5p each. And almost every customer bought half a dozen of them.'

Not only had he implemented Shane's and Karina's ideas, he had refined and improved them even further too.

Clearly, allowing staff like Shane, Karina and Ronan to take risks meant they were able to show their initiative, with brilliant results.

However, this is only part of the story. The truth is, in order to strike gold with one innovation or new idea, you have to be willing to risk several failures first.

In Superquinn, we learned early on that the many successes that came from our willingness to take risks with new ideas repaid the cost of our failures many times over. More precisely, we realised it makes sound business sense to encourage a culture of innovative risk-taking.

One such example of the huge benefits that can come from a willingness to take risks was our successful introduction of in-store bakeries in Superquinn.

The idea came about after I saw a bakery in a hypermarket in Wales during a visit in 1973. The shop was owned by the multinational French company, Carrefour. The bakery was a real focal point of the shop and was doing great trade. It got me thinking, wouldn't it be a great idea to put a full bakery into a shop in Ireland.

So I asked my colleagues to look into ways of doing it.

Mind Your Own Business

Before long, they came up with an implementation plan. In fact, we did it on the cheap at first by buying a chicken rotisserie and using par-baked bread that we got from the famous Boland's Bakery.

The way it worked was that Boland's half-baked the bread, and then we finished it off in the rotisserie in the shop. Most importantly, there was a lovely smell of hot baked bread in the shop, which customers were drawn towards.

When we saw how successful our initial trial of fresh-baked bread was, we decided to go the whole way and introduce in-store bakeries to all of our shops. We opened our first full bakery in Finglas in 1973, a move that represented a significant financial investment for us as a company.

One day I met a customer at 10 a.m. who said, 'When is the fresh bread coming out of the oven?' Now, we were selling some bread baked the day before at about 4 p.m. There was nothing wrong with the bread, it was still fresh. But she added, 'I just love the bread when it's freshly baked,' and I realised I did too.

We decided we would never sell bread more than a few hours old. This meant we had to give away any bread we had left at the end of each day, which made a number of local charities very happy and grateful. We put clocks on our bakeries so customers would know when the breads, cakes, doughnuts or scones were baked, and they were never more than four hours old.

Of course the accountants could not for the life of them see the logic in throwing away perfectly good bread! They pointed out it was very expensive to give the bread away to charity every night.

But our sales rocketed. Within a short time the Finglas bakery was the prototype for a bakery in each of our other shops. And we soon became known as *the* place to go to buy fresh, tasty bread.

Superquinn has also become renowned for the quality of its own-brand sausages, freshly made in-store since 1979. But what many people do not know is that this would never have happened if we did not have a culture within the company that allowed people to risk failing.

One day, Michael O'Connor, an American friend of mine, said to me, 'If you are free on Tuesday, I am bringing some Americans over to Nuremberg to see one of the busiest supermarkets in the world. Why don't you join us?'

So I went along with them. There were four Americans – one with 1,000 stores, one with 700 stores, one with only 200 stores and one with 70 stores. I think I had nine shops at the time, so I was very much a baby among this group of retailers.

When we got to Nuremberg, we visited the most spectacular supermarket I had ever seen. What's more, it operated side by side with a sausage factory. Nuremberg is the sausage centre of the world. There was a glass wall between the two buildings, and people queued up to get the fresh sausages that were being made in front of them behind the glass wall.

You couldn't shop in the supermarket on your own because if you left your trolley somebody would steal the sausages from it — saving themselves the time it would take to queue for the freshly made sausages. They were that popular!

I knew that any shop that could turn its customers into thieves just to get their hands on one of its products (even if they still had to pay for them!) was on to something special. We already had bakeries in every shop, which were doing brilliantly. But Nuremberg got me thinking that a sausage plant in every shop could work equally well.

As we sat around that evening following the visit to the supermarket, I said to the four Americans, 'I can't wait to get home. I think the in-store sausage-making is a smashing idea.'

You see, I had worked out that Maurice in Superquinn Northside would be great at making the sausages, and John in Superquinn Sutton and Jim in Superquinn Finglas came from families that were in the butchery business.

But the Americans with hundreds of stores responded, 'Feargal, we are far too big for that!'

This told me that due to the small size of my company, when compared to those of the Americans on the trip, I knew my staff and knew exactly who amongst them would be best qualified to help me with these plans. I had been reminded that 'small can be beautiful'.

I came back from Nuremberg and said to my colleagues, 'We have got to work at making this new venture a success.'

My colleague Pat Kelly, Regional Manager, pointed out

that we had to make another decision: we could either have the cheapest sausage, the healthiest sausage or the best-tasting sausage. It was another fork-in-the-road moment for Superquinn: the success or failure of the whole project would depend on what we decided to do.

We agreed to focus on taste. We went on to win the 'Sausage of the Year' award for the next number of years.

We received another, rather less official, imprimatur, too. Joan, a customer in our Northside shop, had a dog that would eat no sausages other than Superquinn sausages. When you even mentioned the words 'Superquinn sausages', he wagged his whole rear end (not just his tail)!

This came in particularly handy one time when Joan asked a friend to collect the dog from the kennels. When her friend arrived there, she found it hard to identify Joan's pooch from the others gathered there. She soon solved the problem by saying 'Superquinn sausages' at the top of her voice, before watching as the dog in question immediately wagged his whole rear end. He was obviously a canine with very discerning taste!

It is my firm belief that if we had not been willing to take the risk of trying something new then we would never have sanctioned the huge expense of introducing an in-store bakery to each of our shops. Nor would we have taken the initiative to focus on sausage-making, as the sheer terror of risking failure would have stopped us from doing so.

The same goes for many of the other innovations for which Superquinn became renowned, such as free playhouses for children, salad bars and freshly made in-store pizzas, all of which were a huge success, helping to make Superquinn into the company it is today.

I believe this commitment to innovation is hugely important for all businesses. No matter how large or small, it should be placed firmly at the core of everything you do. Staff should also know it is OK to fail once you learn from it and use it as a springboard to your next big idea.

This is a message worth repeating: for every innovation we got right in Superquinn we got many others wrong. Yet our successes were invariably so worthwhile that our failures were soon forgotten about.

Until now, that is!

11

Of TOGs, DOGs and HOGs

How silent service is key to your business

....

Sammy Ritchie, the manager of Superquinn Naas, pulled me aside one day and pointed to the car park. 'We've had some complaints that the trolleys aren't always as clean as they should be, sometimes the wheels are sticky. I thought it would be good to have someone there to tidy up all the trolleys for an hour each morning,' Sammy said.

'Have a good look at Niall, the guy in charge. He's a seventeen-year-old youngster who came to me looking for work, and I put him on the trolleys to start with.'

I walked outside and watched Niall as the customers came towards him. He greeted them with a very polite, 'Hi, hello, I'm Niall, and my job is to give you a good trolley – here you are.' Then he took out a trolley and studiously checked it.

'Ah,' he said 'that's not good. It's got a wobbly wheel. Sorry about that.'

He put it aside and took another trolley out and said, 'There you go. Oh, wait a minute, there is a cabbage leaf in this one.'

He took another trolley out, which this time was pristine and said, 'There you are now.'

The customer went off very happy.

I'm sure you're asking what did he do with the cabbage leaf?

Well, you're right. He put it back in the next trolley.

And what did he do with the wobbly trolley? He put it back to the front of the trolley line again. When the next customer came up, he would start his 'Hi, I'm Niall, and my job is to give you ...' spiel all over again.

I watched this performance flabbergasted as he did it to customer after customer.

Eventually, I went over and said, 'Niall, what on earth are you up to?'

He replied, 'You wouldn't believe how much the customers appreciate it. If I only left the trolleys ready for use, they wouldn't realise the service we are giving them. Now they appreciate the service.'

Intrigued, I worked on the trolleys for a few minutes myself, and I did the same thing!

I took the first trolley, the wobbly one, and said, 'Sorry that's wobbly, I can't give you that. Let me give you ... Oh, there's a cabbage leaf in that ...' and so on.

I soon realised that it worked a treat!

I gave a trolley to one lady, who thanked me profusely for being so diligent. Later, when I met her in the shop, she turned to her friend and said, 'There's that lovely man I was telling you about. Isn't that a marvellous service they give? They check the trolley before they give it to you.'

Clearly she had not recognised who I was, yet I had made a real impression on her with my trolley-handling abilities!

What's more, Niall told me later that he used a cabbage leaf on Monday, a cigarette pack on Tuesday and a potato-crisp bag on Wednesday!

This example shows the power of allowing space for individual initiative in every business.

As we have discussed already, any healthy business should be focused on fostering a culture of innovation among its employees, although perhaps the above case suggests it can sometimes go a little bit too far.

But it is also vital to realise that businesses can't be creative all of the time. This is why every successful business needs to make room for checklists.

Of course, it would be lovely to think you could get yourself and your staff so fired up that you'd just go in every day and automatically do everything right.

But the reality is, we're all human beings. If you start

> Any healthy business should be focused on fostering a culture of innovation among its employees

from the bottom of the mountain every day, the fact is that some days you'll reach the top.

Other days you won't.

More than ever during a recession, when every penny is being watched nervously, people come to expect certain things from you. If they don't get them, they are disappointed – sometimes very disappointed.

Excellent customer service means, among other things, absolute reliability in what is delivered.

In every business, the problem of how to set and maintain standards is a potentially make-or-break issue: some things simply have to be done without fail if your business is going to be consistently superior to your competitors.

One way of ensuring this is achieved is what I call the McDonald's approach. Everything at McDonald's is systematised, right down to the way customers are greeted. The company has a rule to cover almost every possible eventuality, and all its staff has to do is carry them out.

Clearly there is a large part of customer service that can be set out as a basic standard as in McDonald's.

But I passionately believe that any business looking to truly excel should always be looking to go further than this.

Because if you have the right approach to basic standards they can be a springboard to real and lasting success, no matter the prevailing economic conditions.

Over the course of *Feargal Quinn's Retail Therapy* series, I continuously encountered retailers who had let the standards within their business slip, for a variety of reasons.

In some cases, this had brought them to the brink of ruin during one of the worst recessions the global economy has ever encountered. In my view, the key ingredients many of them were missing were simple: they needed to familiarise themselves with TOGs, DOGs and HOGs!

Let me explain what I mean.

I always say there were two major crisis points for me as a retailer. The first was when I went from owning one shop to opening a second outlet.

This was because it meant that I had to really learn the importance of trusting my managers and employees with my business as I would no longer be on hand to personally supervise everything that went on in my shop.

By this, I mean having confidence that everybody who worked with me had the same enthusiasm and anxiety to excel as I did.

And I was lucky to be able to rely on some truly brilliant people to help me on my early business journey.

The next big crisis occurred when we went from six to seven shops. At this stage, I just knew I had to put some sort of formalised structure to my business.

When there were only two or three (or even five) shops, each manager could pick up the telephone and call me with any query. I was also able to spend the best part of a day in each shop every week, to see how things were on the ground.

As the company expanded, it was just not possible for me to do this. I needed to set the tone for my business while also making sure that the simple things were being done well.

This is what I like to call silent service – the vital work that goes on behind the scenes to make sure customers are given the very best service.

At Superquinn, one of the key ways we did this was by introducing a variety of different checklists for our staff to use.

When Quinn's Supermarket opened in Dundalk back in 1960, my six staff and I spent the first three days of the week getting the shop ready for the busy weekend.

On Thursday evening, we would not go home until the shop floor was in great nick. We had a checklist that we called the Thursday Order Guide.

But of course we did not call it that: for us, it was always known as the TOG.

Some years later, as the company began to expand, we discovered that having the shops in a good state once a week was no longer good enough.

While it was great to make sure our shops were in tip-top shape in advance of the busy weekend period, we knew other customers arriving into Superquinn earlier in the week were just as entitled to expect an excellent standard of service as our weekend customers.

We established the Daily Order Guide – the DOG – to ensure certain basic standards were being met on a daily basis too. It had just six points on it and was very simple to use. (More on this below.)

The DOG actually came about (or barked for the first time!) following a conversation I had in Superquinn Blackrock with Vincent Martin, the specialist in charge of all our butchery departments.

I asked Vincent how he spent his week. 'I visit all the branches to see that everything is in good order,' he replied.

'Could I help you?' I asked. 'Suppose there's something wrong in one of those shops, which will not be identified and fixed until you get there. Could those of us who are visiting the shops, or somebody else in the shop, help you to make sure that everything is OK, even when you are not there?'

'You would need to serve your time as an apprentice to become a Master Butcher,' he responded, 'and that takes five years.'

At that very moment I noticed a customer looking for something at the pre-pack section. She wanted three pork chops but only packs of two and four were on display – we had sold out of the one and three packs. 'Vincent,' I said, 'even someone who is not a skilled butcher could check that.'

And he agreed.

We talked about it some more and realised there were some jobs that Vincent was doing personally, such as checking the sell-by date on fresh produce and making sure there was enough of each product on display, which could be done by anyone at the shop.

From that point on we made out a very simple checklist for all of the butchery staff to use.

Then we went to the fish specialist, Tommy Spratt, and asked him to make a similar list. Our aim was to make it so simple that even an inexperienced sixteen-year-old on his or her first day in the job could do it.

The types of things Tommy's list looked for were 'Is there a mussel that's open?' and 'Is there a speck of blood on the salmon?'

You can probably guess by now what happened next. We did the same with the fruit and vegetable department, and then with the delicatessen and pizza department. And so on.

We were delighted with ourselves as we saw the real difference that DOGs were making to our business.

That is, until we found that the DOG simply wasn't good enough, either.

This was because, although the shop floor could be ready at 9 a.m. through the use of a DOG, it would be in disarray again by 2 p.m.

And this is when the baby of the bunch, and the DOG's youngest brother, the Hourly Order Guide (or HOG) was born.

It is no exaggeration to say that the HOG transformed the way we did things at Superquinn.

By allowing staff to operate off what some people might think of as boring checklists of things to look out for, they could be sent out two or three times a day, or more, to make sure everything on this list was being ticked off.

I suggested to John Foy, manager of Superquinn Blanchardstown, that he should use a HOG. He complained that the company was becoming far too bureaucratic. But I explained the rationale behind it: 'John, this is a way of guaranteeing that all these simple things are looked after. You don't have to put yourself or a senior manager on it. You get a young person to go around every morning at 10 a.m., so the department have until 10 a.m. to get ready. Then they go around again at 2 p.m. or whatever time it is.'

And do you know what? About six weeks later John said to me, 'Feargal, I criticised the paperwork but it is actually the most useful tool I have found for managing. Things that were going wrong before don't go wrong anymore. Because the head butcher, for example, knows there's someone coming around regularly to check things and ensure everything is perfect.'

Crucially, it also meant that the head butcher was doing the things he should be doing rather than spending too much of his time unnecessarily on these small but important things.

The key to our TOGs, DOGs and HOGs was they were very simple to understand. But they were also quite detailed, setting out the things that must happen as a matter of course.

No discussion, no initiative, no creativity. The message to our staff was clear: these things had to be addressed, no matter what.

You know when a pilot is about to take off? You don't expect him to use his imagination or creativity. You expect him to go carefully through the pre-take-off checklist. He doesn't have to rely on his memory, or how he's feeling – he just has to do the checklist.

Well, with customer service in business it's the same.

In Superquinn, we always viewed checklists as a platform, the springboard for individual initiative. We still desperately wanted the Nialls of this world to feel they could devise their own ways of doing things that would add to the customer experience.

Similarly, Shane with his kumquats, which we referred to in Chapter 10, also needed to know that a major part of his job was to do the simple things brilliantly. This could then act as a baseline from which his powers of innovation could soar.

If you like, checklists are the cake onto which we could put the icing. But if the cake itself is not there, nobody's going to be impressed by icing on its own.

The lesson for every business is that you and your staff cannot be creative all the time.

So you must always leave room for your very own TOGs, DOGs and HOGs, too.

12

Become a true destination

Why your customers should always pass your competitors

....

I am convinced, now more than ever, that every shop, business or retailer needs to be the best at something it does. They need to become a destination for their customers.

During an economic downturn, the logic behind this is pretty obvious: if you can get a sufficient number of customers to choose your shop or service above others, then you stand an excellent chance of weathering the current financial storms.

One business that has learned what it takes to become a destination is X-It Department Store in Finglas. But it was not always this way.

Every shop, business or retailer needs to be the best at something it does

To truly understand how X-It made this vital transition, we must first of all talk about the Joy of Onions.

I went into a supermarket in Texas some years ago. The store itself was perfectly nice, if rather unremarkable – until I saw its glorious onions, that is. Now, these onions were just magnificent. They looked absolutely world-class, sitting there on the supermarket display. There were all types of onions available, and each of the different varieties had its own separate mini-display area. They were fresh, inviting ... and looked darned tasty too.

So much so that if there was somebody in the area who was really fussy about onions, I would wager they would have little choice but to go to that particular store for their onion fix.

What's more, even if you happened to only like onions, this store's specimens were so appealing you would probably want to bring some of them home, regardless of whether they were on your original shopping list when you first entered the store.

To put it another way, I did not need to spend my time passionately contributing to online discussion boards about the Joy of Onions, nor be a member of an onion fan club to really appreciate what this store in Texas was offering.

This is the key to becoming a true destination retailer: if any shop can make one or more of its products or services so appealing that the fussy enthusiast will want to come

there, they will win their custom.

An excellent by-product of this is that others from the more general customer population will appreciate what is being offered and will most likely choose that shop over its competitors because they appreciate the quality of what is being offered, too.

Thoroughly impressed by the onions I had seen in Texas, I returned home and asked my colleagues how we could become the onion centre of Ireland. We then set about making sure that Superquinn became one of the best places in Ireland to buy onions.

I have singled out onions, but, of course, the same could be said of any other fresh produce – or, indeed, of any other non-branded product in your shop.

There is always somebody out there who would kill for onions. It might only be 5 per cent of the population, but there might be another 5 per cent who would kill for mushrooms, and probably another 5 per cent who would kill for tomatoes.

At Superquinn, we also asked could we become the mushroom centre of Ireland, could we become the tomato centre of Ireland? And so on.

That's what I call the logic of being a destination business: there is always somebody out there who says, 'I will drive past another dozen shops because I am mad keen on onions.'

In Chapter 10, I told the story of how we came to offer freshly baked bread in all of our Superquinn shops. But the only reason this happened was because we asked the question, 'How will we be the best at bread?' From this, we got the idea of introducing in-shop ovens at Superquinn, making us a destination for fresh bread in Ireland. It soon became very clear that people were driving past other supermarkets to come to us just for our bread.

We did not stop there. Having established one key selling point, we looked around for others that would make us even more attractive to potential customers. We asked, 'Could we do the same with sausages?'

What we were aiming for was real destination shopping. We knew that if somebody was really enthusiastic about sausages they would drive past our competitors to get these tasty sausages that were only available from us.

Then we did the same with salads and with other products such as in-shop pizzas, because we knew that every time we succeeded we were winning over another swathe of loyal customers.

In business, it is vital to ask yourself, 'Will what we are offering bring people not just from the neighbourhood, but past our competitors to shop here?'

That was the question we continuously asked ourselves when it came to ensuring we were a destination shop.

For example, when we opened shops in areas of Dublin such as Sutton, one fear we had was that there were not enough people living in the immediate neighbourhood for us to become a sustainable neighbourhood shop. We knew from the start that we simply had to coax people from surrounding areas such as Baldoyle, Raheny and Clontarf.

In order to do this, we had to continuously focus on becoming a destination shop for them. We did this through the quality of our offering and, of course, the customer service we provided once they came inside.

Over time, we became the best in Ireland at bakery products, the best in Ireland at sausages, the best in Ireland at salads, and the best in Ireland at pizzas.

This was because when we set our minds to offering our customers a new product, we didn't want to provide it unless we were the best.

I remember vividly a customer who attended a customer panel in our Blackrock shop. When a question popped up about Quinnsworth's Merrion shop, one of our rival shops in the area, the customer said, 'I was there once but I felt guilty at the checkout.'

I asked her, 'Why on earth did you feel guilty?'

She said, 'One time in Superquinn Bray I came to the checkout and my bill came to about £80. But I realised when I had gone through the checkout and packed everything that I had left my purse at home by mistake. I said to the checkout operator, "Will you put my food aside and I will be back with the money to pay for the goods?" I asked would they put the frozen food in the freezer and the ice cream in the ice-cream cabinet, and I would be back in forty-five minutes.

'The manager, Damien Kiernan, said, "I tell you what: take them with you, and the next time you are in you can pay for them." Ever since that day I have felt guilty if I shopped anywhere else.'

It wasn't that she just felt guilty shopping at Quinnsworth: it was anywhere other than at Superquinn. She felt a sense of obligation after she had been treated so well in our shop by Damien.

The amazing thing was that Damien had left that shop fourteen years before to manage our Blackrock shop! For fourteen years she had felt guilty shopping anywhere else, solely because one of our managers had trusted her.

This struck me as being hugely important: on the basis of that trust she was willing to pass other shops just to repay us. My next thought was how could I make every customer feel as guilty – or, in other words, as loyal – as she felt.

When we first visited husband-and-wife team Derek and Fionnuala Law as part of the *Feargal Quinn's Retail Therapy* series, they had been operating their small discount shop, X-It Department Store, out of Finglas Main Centre for eighteen years. To start with, business was good, and they employed several staff.

There were plans to rebuild the shopping centre as part of the property boom, but since the recession there were a number of empty units in the centre. In all honesty, X-It seemed quite run down too, with dated fixtures and fittings.

Apart from Fionnuala's and Derek's warm personalities, there were two important positives for X-It: the Finglas

Library was overhead, and X-It shared the shopping centre with the local post office. As a result, there were many people coming in and out of the centre. Unfortunately, these potential customers never darkened X-It's doors, meaning this was a real missed opportunity.

The first time I went to visit the shop in Finglas, I couldn't even find it. I went into the Finglas Main Centre and walked up and down looking for the shop. Finally someone spotted me, took pity upon me and asked what I was looking for. They drew my attention to a small sign in the corner with X-It written up on it.

My first impression was that this sign was showing me the way out of the centre. There was no evidence of a shop window there, nor indeed any sign of a shop. It was a case of location, location, location ... gone wrong.

There was a blank wall on one side of the shop. On the other side was the busy post office, with queues frequently out the door. This meant the shop effectively had a captive audience who had no idea of what was in the shop right beside them.

I asked could we put windows into this wall so that people could see across to the shop. This would allow Derek and Fionnuala to use these windows to display their wares. After all, if you are stuck in a queue, you are going to look around you. It is just what you do.

When you go shopping you usually have a list, mental or otherwise, of what you want to get. One item on it will spark off another thing you want in that general area.

For example, tea will remind you of sugar, milk or coffee. And in the back of your mind there are a couple of other things you intend getting but which haven't actually made it onto your list.

X-It could potentially profit by providing some of these goods. If you are looking for a birthday card, there's a good chance you are holding a birthday celebration or will be attending one. If there's a birthday party planned, you might also want decorations, candles, balloons, streamers, etc. I knew that if X-It could make a name for itself as a shop that specialised in these types of items, it could become the first port of call for anyone planning a birthday.

Another way of putting this is that it would be a destination shop, with customers travelling there for their party goods rather than trying to pull together bits and pieces from half a dozen non-specialised shops.

In making this market niche for itself, X-It would also be building up a long-term customer base which would be broadened by positive word of mouth. As I have already noted in Chapter 3, this is the best form of advertising that money can't buy.

It was clear to me that we needed to make X-It a destination shop, by encouraging its customers to show it their loyalty.

We knew that X-It had a reputation for offering the best-value greetings cards in town. Retailing at two cards for €1, they were not generating enough money.

The key was to look at ways of providing add-on products. These would serve two purposes: they would encourage those customers who already shopped in X-It for their greeting cards to buy additional goods, thereby increasing the average spend.

They would also make new or only occasional shoppers think of X-It in a different way, as somewhere to go for items they had not realised to be on sale there previously. From this was born the idea of making the shop a destination for celebrations – a one-stop party shop, for want of a better word.

One of the best ways of ensuring you become a true destination for your customers is by going the extra mile to make their lives as easy as possible.

During one of our regular Superquinn customer-panel meetings, someone expressed annoyance at something that had happened at one of our competitor's shops. The bill came to £15.01. He had £20 but not the penny, so he had to take £4.99 in change.

This was just one of many comments at what was a pretty typical customer panel. Nevertheless, we fed it back to our staff.

The following week, when I went back in to one of our branches, I found Ray Clarke, the manager, had put a little saucer on every one of the sixteen checkouts. He had put six pennies in each saucer with a little sign saying, 'Take a penny, leave a penny'.

You would not believe the amount of praise we got from customers who just couldn't believe that they were now never going to be burdened with unnecessary change.

> One of the best ways of ensuring you become a true destination for your customers is by going the extra mile to make their life as easy as possible

Under the 'saucer system', if your bill came to, say, £4.01 or even £4.02, then the checkout operator could just point to the saucer and tell you to take the penny or tuppence you needed from it.

This has always seemed to me to be something so simple; there was nothing high-tech about it whatsoever. But every customer who benefited from the penny saucer would be a missionary for Superquinn by telling others about it.

It also frequently paid for itself, too.

Ray counted his pennies at the end of the day and found that while he started with £1 he often had more than £1 left over. It transpired that most people don't want pennies in their pocket and so they tended to leave them there. In return for helping our customers, and generating goodwill, sometimes we ended up with more pennies than we started out with.

It is one thing to decide what is going to be your destination product or service, what will make people drive to you ahead of your competitors. But this is not enough on its own.

It is even more important that you do whatever it takes to ensure you continue to be the best at what you do.

Throughout my career at Superquinn we continually expanded the company. At the same time, we were always interested in investing in our business and always looking at ways of pushing it forward. This impulse to challenge ourselves was very clearly linked to the idea of continuing to be a destination for our customers.

One good litmus test we employed was to ask ourselves constantly, 'How can we say that a product we are selling is going to ensure we are the destination of choice for somebody who is fussy about that product?'

All businesses, no matter their size, have to strive to be dynamic every day of every week. This is true regardless of whether there is a recession or not. As far back as 1965, when we opened our Finglas shop, we were asking ourselves, 'What will we do next week? What have we got?'

This comes back to the idea of creating a sense of excitement around your business, which in turn feeds into making it a destination shop.

And whether it was 'we will burst balloons', or 'we will have a raffle', or 'we will have you win your weight in groceries', we desperately wanted those customers to come to our shop. There is no use having the best shop in the world if no one comes inside.

I remember trying to get publicity for our Sutton shop when it opened in 1968. I went to Fossett's Circus and asked, 'Could you bring an elephant along?' And we brought the elephant. It was a big story that the supermarket was being opened by our pachydermal dignitary – unfortunately he was not house-trained!

A food shop bringing an elephant in, even if he was only a baby elephant, generated the type of publicity we simply couldn't pay for.

In Ancient Rome, the Forum was the centre of public and commercial life in the city. It was where local traders and business people gathered to swap goods, trades and services.

But it was also the focal point for much of the city's political life too. For example, an individual seeking to make his pitch to the local townsfolk would do so by standing on a plinth in the Forum and making a public speech.

This idea of a major commercial hub being the centre point of the community has not completely gone away in more modern times, either.

Back in 1969, I was working in our Sutton shop when the eminent historian, author and politician Conor Cruise O'Brien rushed over to me to tell me he had just been thrown out of my shop!

It was general-election time, and he was going around the shop shaking hands with constituents, much as I imagine political candidates in Roman times would have done in the Forum.

He was spotted by the shop manager, John Gunnigle, who approached him to insist that he was not to come into the shop canvassing for votes.

Conor was thoroughly unimpressed with this. As he explained, 'I have been to the United Nations, I have travelled around the world ... and I have never been treated like this. We should have a right to speak to our constituents.'

I agreed with Conor – to a point. While local politicians should be able to talk to their constituents, I also felt their constituents should be able to do their shopping in peace, if they so wished.

Then I had an idea: wouldn't it be great if we could make Superquinn in Sutton into the local Forum for the north-east Dublin area? I booked a huge trailer, and we put it into the Superquinn car park. I invited all of the local politicians to address their constituents on the following Friday. And they all turned up, including Conor and Charles J. Haughey, who later went on to become Taoiseach.

The car park was packed. And you can imagine my delight when I saw that our Superquinn event, which placed us at the heart of our community, made the front page of the *Irish Independent* newspaper the following day.

All of these types of stunts generated huge word-of-mouth publicity for us and reinforced us as a destination retailer in the local area. They meant that when Mrs Murphy met Mrs or Mr Smith, who lived a mile away, she would say, 'Do you know what they are doing in Superquinn this week? Do you know what they are doing?' to the extent that people felt obliged to come down just to see.

Each of the retailers we visited during *Feargal Quinn's Retail Therapy* needed to address their *destination deficit*, as I like to call it, in one way or another. Sometimes when I tried to suggest big ideas, they would say to us, 'But this is what we've always done, and, you know, why do we have to do something new this week?'

I tried always to convince them that change and innovation needed to be a core part of what they did so that somebody waking up in the morning would say, 'I wonder what's going on down there today? It's Monday morning, I wonder what's happening?'

I know how lucky I am to have grown up in a holiday camp, where the emphasis was on continually keeping our guests entertained, with a view to winning their repeat custom. The idea of constantly innovating was ingrained in me from an early age.

But this approach can be learned too, once retailers and business people are willing to embrace the change in mentality this requires.

I sometimes like to compare it to the difference between Billy and Bob. Billy has a party and the next day doesn't get out of bed because he is so exhausted. He goes on to spend the week cleaning up and complaining about how wrecked he is from the exertions of the night.

But Bob's mentality is different: he too is exhausted after he finishes the party. But his immediate reaction is to say, 'Gosh that was great, I must have another one.'

We see similar traits in successful sportspeople too, people who are invariably extremely goal-oriented. Very often, when you hear soccer stars, such as the Republic of Ireland soccer legend Roy Keane, talk about their careers, they place very little emphasis on the joy of celebrating winning a league title or a major cup.

Instead, they talk about the enjoyment of setting themselves a goal, achieving the goal and waking up the next morning and saying, 'How do I do that again?'

In business, in order to survive and prosper, as soon as you reach one peak you need to say, 'OK, so where's my next mountain to climb?'

Of course, Superquinn is far from being alone in recognising the need to create a sense of excitement around its products. One of the most successful Irish companies of recent years is the airline Ryanair, whose flamboyant chief executive Michael O'Leary certainly does whatever it takes to make sure his company generates headlines.

This has included dressing up as a highwayman to protest against fuel surcharges, donning a Santa Claus outfit to publicise a Christmas sale, becoming a gondolier to push cheap flights to Venice and even channelling his inner St Patrick to coincide with Ireland's national holiday.

Now, his approach to customer service would be somewhat different to mine, of course. But, regardless, O'Leary is a good example of a businessman who clearly identified early on in his career at Ryanair just how important it was to make sure his company was featuring in the minds of its customers, through his innovative publicity stunts.

Another good example of this is the Irish bookmaker, Paddy Power, which offers a huge range of novelty bets in response to the talking points of the day as a way of upping its company profile. Coupled with frequently cheeky advertisements, the company manages to push itself to the forefront of punters' minds at all times.

It is also surely no coincidence that the hugely successful German discount retailers Aldi and Lidl start each week with extensive print-based advertisements and brochures highlighting new and inexpensive special offers in their shops.

These range from cheap skiing or camping gear to garden furniture, men's clothing and household DIY items. The sheer variety is constantly surprising.

Again, this is all about creating a sense of curiosity amongst their customers, who are constantly wondering what new bargain or special offer they will find in their shops.

All of the above are types of destination marketing: making sure that potential customers actively want to go to their shops or to avail of their products.

Some two years after we had first worked with X-It, I pulled into the car park of Finglas Main Centre with no small degree of apprehension.

As I was driving, I was speaking to camera. I actually said, 'I am not really confident because I fear they may have returned to the standards that were there before we arrived.'

My mood was not helped when I saw, two years on, the shopping centre still had many vacant units. How would X-It fare?

My fears were completely unfounded. I could not have been more thrilled when I entered the shop.

The shop is now selling higher-value cards as well as the cheaper ones — Fionnuala and Derek had clearly realised they needed to cater to the wider greeting-card market. While X-It is an excellent place to buy lower-priced cards, the shop can also give you a more upmarket selection.

They have opened a christening section; they have expanded the toy section; and they have done a good job on what I call the celebration section, which caters not just for birthdays but for events such as hen parties and stag nights, too.

Even more remarkable for me was the transformation in Derek and Fionnuala themselves. They were now both full of energy and enthusiasm.

At one stage, Fionnuala told me her participation in the show had put a mirror in front of her as to the state of the shop. She said that for the first time ever she saw it for what it was.

I also asked Derek, 'What was the one lesson you learned from your participation in the show?'

His response excited me hugely: 'To be great at something,' he said.

Fionnuala and Derek have worked incredibly hard to maintain the standards we had worked on during the television series. I was very impressed at the price and range of the goods on offer in X-It.

But they did not stop there; they were already working away at becoming a destination shop for a second, completely different type of product: school uniforms.

This section of the shop had been in existence for some years but was not performing as well as it should. The way it works is that they buy the school jumpers, pinafores and other items already made up and then they sew on the crest of the school for their customers – at roughly half the price of some other shops.

Again, this seriously impressed me, as it showed that Derek and Fionnuala were no longer happy just to sit still. Instead, they were looking to constantly improve their shop.

When we were leaving the shop later on that day, we met a customer who had just shopped there. As we walked over towards Superquinn Finglas with her, I asked, 'Are you a regular?'

She said, 'No.'

It transpired that she had gone elsewhere at first to buy a school uniform for her daughter and was surprised at the price. Then somebody told her it was a lot cheaper in X-It, which was why she had shopped there.

The equation of that conversation sums up destination logic perfectly. Let's call it Feargal's Destination Theorem:

word-of-mouth recommendation + quality and value of goods on sale = X-It as a destination shop

Sometimes, I just love maths.

13

Overcoming the hand of history

Respecting tradition while valuing innovation

....

I want to let you into a little secret. Perhaps it is not something you may have thought about me.

Whisper it: sometimes I like nothing more than when someone disagrees with me.

There. I've said it.

Now don't tell anyone.

I was reminded of this when I met Cliona Standún, the young, vivacious managing director of Standún Clothing and Giftware shop in rural An Spidéal, Connemara.

As someone who had only recently taken over her family's long-established business, Cliona was clearly bright, enthusiastic and willing to embrace change in the hope of helping to secure the future of the shop. And she was certainly no pushover.

Standún is an iconic shop in the Connemara Gaeltacht, well known by generations of locals and tourists alike as a clothing and giftware shop. But it desperately needed to attract more Irish visitors and foreign tourists while at the same time managing to not alienate its existing clientele. This can be a tricky challenge for even the most accomplished of jugglers.

When I first arrived at Standún, truth be told, I was underwhelmed by the outside of the shop. It did nothing to excite my interest about what I would find inside. I was similarly unimpressed by the fact that no one greeted me when I entered the shop. Its signage appeared confused and unclear, failing to clearly tell customers where things were to be found.

For example, its coffee bar and toilets were located at the back of the shop. But you would not know this from the in-store signs. This meant that Cliona and her team were missing a vital opportunity to showcase their products to the busloads of tourists stopping by.

So, I came up with one of my 'big ideas'. This was to have Cliona commission the biggest Irish flag in the whole of Ireland, something I felt would make the shop a major talking point on the tourist trail.

My thinking was we should seek to make Standún *the* tourist shop in Connemara, a place where any one of the many thousands of people who visit this most picturesque of areas simply *had* to go to for their Irish memorabilia.

Buoyed by my 'big idea', and confidently expecting Cliona to be equally as enthusiastic about my plan to make the shop more tourist-centric, I approached her to outline my views.

I was met with a big, fat, firm 'No!' in response.

Despite her youth and relative inexperience, Cliona was confident enough in her own vision for the shop to tell me that my idea was just not a goer. The flag idea was, she felt passionately, too touristy, too gimmicky.

Instead, she believed the shop needed to work at better identifying the needs of 'staycationers', or Irish tourists, who were not travelling abroad as much because of the recession. This had led to a flood of excellent-value hotel deals enticing people to indulge in mini-breaks in places just like Connemara.

Coupled with this, she wanted to see the shop move more towards the fashion market, to make it a good place for people in the locality to come for their clothes.

Of course, I did not necessarily agree with her. After all, the giant flag was my brilliant idea in the first place!

But I did respect the fact that she stood by the courage of her convictions in telling me where to put my plans. By showing me she was willing to listen to my suggestions, while also saying why she felt they were just plain wrong, I was left in little doubt as to who would be making the final decisions from now on.

And I could not have been happier with this situation.

Standún had been run by Cliona's father Donal since 1973, when he took it over from his own father. Donal and his wife Raymonde still play an active part on a day-to-day basis and are always on hand to provide practical advice and support to their daughter when needed.

And herein lay another potential problem that I have seen time and again in family-run businesses, including my own.

How do you allow your offspring or management the space to breathe new life and ideas into your business while also ensuring the business does not lose what made it survive down the generations in the first place?

Or, more simply, how do you preserve what makes it special while enabling it to change with the times?

I like to call this Overcoming the Hand of History. It is about respecting tradition while valuing innovation.

There are many other more subtle ways in which the hand of history can weigh heavily on the shoulders of a business owner.

For example, Denis Murphy at the BMC convenience shop in Cobh, Co. Cork, told us early on in *Feargal Quinn's Retail Therapy* series that he was afraid of letting down the past generations of his family who had toiled to make the shop a viable enterprise.

He had been carrying on the family tradition passed down from his father and grandfather all of his working life. The weight of this responsibility meant an eighty-hour working week for him in the face of increased competition from multinational and German discount stores.

As a third-generation owner of the shop, he was understandably very conscious of the shop's heritage. As he put it, 'I don't want to mess this place up and have it close when it's under my ownership.'

But at what point does this all-too-understandable fear of 'messing up' a long-established business become something else? What if it becomes a barrier to taking the necessary steps to secure the very future of your business?

The problem is, of course, that it can be all too easy to live in your customers' past and not in their present. What a customer wanted two decades (or even two days) ago is not necessarily what they want today.

This reminds me of the old Irish proverb 'Éist le ruaim na h-abhann is gheobhaidh tú iasc', which translated means 'Listen to the sound of the river and you will catch a fish.'

The reason you need to listen to the sound of the river is because the water in the river is not the same this week as it was last week. And it certainly is not the same as it was last year or five, ten or twenty years ago.

Just as the water in the river is constantly changing, so the marketplace is changing all of the time too. And you've got to listen to it, because even if you just want to stand still in business you have to keep moving.

Time and again I have seen at first hand how business has a knack of changing, just when your back is turned.

> What a customer wanted two decades (or even two days) ago is not necessarily what they want today

Clearly, you want to hold on to tradition and history. But there must always be a firm business case for doing so.

In other words, maintaining a keen sense of your company's history is important. But it always has to be of benefit to your business to do so. By the same token, it is vitally important, no matter how well your business is doing, that you keep responding to your customers' *current* needs.

Put simply, you have to continually move with the times. Otherwise, there is a real danger that you will become stuck in a rut.

This may well masquerade as a respect for tradition, for the way things have always been done. But, just like bread on the shelves of a bakery, tradition can become stale with time, discouraging current and potential customers alike from ever darkening the doors of your business again.

So beware the old ways of doing things – and don't just do what Granddad did.

Let me give you an example from my own family history.

In 1936, my father, Eamonn Quinn, who had been to the USA ten years earlier, was working with his father. Grandfather John Quinn had three grocery shops in Dublin called Quinn's: in Dun Laoghaire, Moore Street and Drumcondra.

The business wasn't doing as well as it should have been, and my father argued with his father that in America you would be more competitive by cutting prices. But Grandfather Quinn said, 'It is unethical to cut the price, you should compete on service and quality.'

Such an approach might seem downright strange in today's marketplace. But in those days this was the norm for busi-

Just like bread on the shelves of a bakery, tradition can become stale with time, discouraging current and potential customers alike

nesses that sold essential everyday goods and provisions to their clientele.

My grandfather was only articulating what was a widely held belief at the time. My father sensed things in the marketplace were about to change and argued that Quinn's needed to be ahead of the curve.

While he had a deep loyalty and respect for his own father, and for the tradition he had used to such good effect in building up his business, my father also glimpsed an opportunity to branch out on his own. He did this by opening Payantake, a shop in Kilmainham.

Unlike most traditional shops, it was based on a 'cash and carry' model. There was no credit, no delivery, and you had to pay for your jams, meat, tea, etc., at each department till. Needless to say, this was a radical departure in the marketplace.

Because there was no credit and no delivery service, the costs were low so prices could be more competitive than other shops using the more traditional 'full service' model of business.

And do you know what?

Payantake thrived, purely because my father was willing to break from tradition by competing on price, something that in those days was unheard of. In so doing, he helped to set new standards in Irish retailing that, within a short period of time, had themselves become commonplace.

This story shows that the 'norms' in business can change, regardless of the current way of doing things. Nothing, and I mean nothing, is set in stone when it comes to delivering excellent service to your customers.

This is something I have been acutely aware of throughout my own career in retailing too. Let me give you another example, this one from my time in the supermarket trade. When you think of Superquinn, I would hope you think of customer service, first and foremost. But it might surprise you to learn, back in 1960 when we opened in Dundalk, we were not known for service at all.

We were actually a 'self-service' shop, meaning that customers were – gasp! – expected to fetch and select their own shopping from our shelves. Up until we opened our doors, the accepted norm in Irish food retailing was for the staff in the shop to do this for the customer, either at the butcher's counter, or at a service counter for tea, or bread, etc.

Even when my father opened Payantake, with its radical new emphasis on cost competitiveness, it continued to provide these service counters to its customers. I vividly recall a member of a prominent Dundalk family coming into our Quinn's Dundalk shop one day to do her shopping, not long after we had opened.

'My husband said you are a young man starting up a business and I should give you a turn,' she told me rather imperiously.

There was one small problem: she had never been in a self-service shop before. I took a basket off the rack to give her, but she didn't take it from me. And this was not the type of woman you argued with easily! Despite my best intentions, I found myself walking around the shop with her, which wasn't the idea at all.

> Nothing, and I mean nothing, is set in stone when it comes to delivering excellent service to your customers

As we went around, she pointed out what foodstuffs she wanted: 'I'll have one of those, two of that,' she said. When she had filled one basket, I dutifully got another basket. By the time she came to the checkout, she asked if I had her address for delivery. Again, this is what she would have expected in any other grocery shop in the town.

At this stage, I simply had to break the awful news to her.

'We don't actually deliver; we don't have transport,' I said, somewhat sheepishly. 'But,' I added, 'we can get somebody to go down to your car with you ... Oh, and we don't do credit, you pay cash.'

Well, you can imagine her reaction. She was stunned. She ended up writing a cheque for her food before leaving the shop with a look of quiet bafflement on her face.

But do you know what?

The next time she came in, she was happy to play by the new rules, as we had established them. And she became a very good customer.

The reason I tell this story is because everyone else gave much more service than we did when we first opened our doors in Dundalk. They gave credit, you paid at the end of the month, and they delivered to your home and did the shopping for you, at counters dotted around the shop.

We told our customers, politely, to take a basket when they came through our doors. And you were expected to go around and do your own shopping. You paid cash, and you carried your goods home.

Clearly, what we were offering was actually far less service than our competitors. Surely there was some mistake here and we were doomed?

Quite the opposite transpired. Within a few years, many of our competitors who stuck rigidly with the traditional ways of doing things were no longer around. Meanwhile, we were thriving and went on to open new shops around the country.

The reason? We had redefined what service was, regardless of the tradition. The new type of service we were giving was based not just on lower prices but also on offering customers the opportunity to select their own food.

You see, up until that point, customers were reliant on an intermediary, the shop assistant, to pick out their goods for them. But we cut out the middleman, so customers were able to pick up and examine their items before buying – a hugely positive development for the customer (if not for some of my competitors).

In *Crowning the Customer*, I told the story of a customer who went into Lipton's and said, 'I want a quarter pound of tea.'

'Do you want the gold tea for two shillings and sixpence, the silver tea for two shillings, the bronze tea for one shilling and sixpence or do you really want that cheap tea for one shilling?' they would be asked.

As a result, customers were often embarrassed to buy the cheapest tea.

But if you went into Quinn's supermarket, under our new service model, you could just buy the tea without any embarrassment. You did not have to wait for an intermediary to ask you for your selection, though staff were on hand if you needed guidance.

Interestingly, the item we sold a lot of was cheap toilet rolls – the thruppence hal'penny kind – because it turned out people were shy about going in and asking for less expensive toilet rolls from an attentive shopkeeper.

Of course, when people spoke about Superquinn during my time with the company they would regularly say things to me like, 'Oh, you changed things. You gave great service, you packed the bags, and you looked after our children and everything else.'

Whereas in fact we offered a different kind of service to that of our competitors. But we had identified what we thought would suit the market *at that time*.

The lesson in this is that there clearly is a benefit in maintaining the standards that the previous generation have espoused. But, at times, it is also vital that you are willing to challenge tradition too.

This is an approach we tried to foster down through the years in Superquinn. For example, we were the first supermarket in Ireland to introduce internet shopping. Again, this was virtually unheard of in the Irish marketplace at the time.

Later, we extended this by developing a collection service for customers who found they were time-poor and wanted to avoid the hassle of picking out their own food. This was called *Click and Collect*. With this service, you did your shopping on the Internet. We picked out your groceries, and we had it waiting for you in three different food cabins: frozen, chilled and ambient.

When you came down to collect your goods after work, we had done the shopping for you. All of these innovations came about as a result of really listening to our customers.

But they also came from our fundamental willingness to break from tradition in the pursuit of a better customer experience.

In Cliona at Standún, we had a young woman with a strong sense of the tradition her family had built up over many years of successful trading in Connemara.

But, as I said earlier, she was also clear in her vision as to where she wanted the company to go. This was not about forgetting all that had gone before but rather about identifying new possibilities *for the future*.

One major way she did this during the show was by listening to her customers and registering what it was they really wanted from her shop. She did not want the shop to be identified simply as a traditional tourist shop with just traditional Irish Aran sweaters. Rather, she felt there was a place for Standún to become a Brown Thomas or Harvey Nichols type of shop for the entire Connemara region. This could cater to the newly resurgent 'staycation' market, as well as the people of Galway who were interested in buying fashionable goods.

Cliona's vision for the shop would take it in a very different direction to the one I had originally suggested. But I was delighted to help her in her efforts, safe in the knowledge that she had a keen vision for the family business, based on her own gut instinct.

Ultimately, Cliona pursued her own path with Standún.

And, thankfully, it has been a success. Takings are up since the show was broadcast, and she tells me that many of the changes we introduced are encouraging new customers into the shop, while making the shopping experience easier for its existing tourist clientele.

Cliona has also embraced email marketing in a very clever way. By its nature, Standún attracts overseas customers who very often only visit the shop once in their lifetime as they tour Ireland. Cliona sees this not as a challenge but as an opportunity. Every overseas customer who visits Standún is asked for permission to email them when they get back home.

By so doing, Cliona is ensuring that only those who actually want to hear from her shop will get an email, and they will not view the contact from Standún as annoying (and very negative) spam mail.

The email they receive provides details of Standún's online shopping facility to these former customers of the shop. Cliona also sends the occasional email at seasonal times, reminding this group of some of the gift ideas from her shop, opening up yet another potential avenue for Standún to generate new sales.

It is worth noting that a major factor in the many positive developments at Standún since we visited with the *Retail Therapy* series was the attitude of Cliona's father, Donal, to the process. At all times, he was willing to respect her ideas and capacity for leadership while also remaining on hand to offer advice and support.

Despite having run the shop since 1973, Donal was confident about handing over control and decision-making to Cliona. He trusted her judgement. He could not have chosen a better person: an individual whose strong personality meant she would not let anyone, or anything, prevent her from introducing her vision for the company. Even a wise(ned) old supermarket boss, like me!

14

Take precautions

The importance of responsible family planning

....

The sound of raucous laughter emanating from the little old lady in the supermarket aisle was unmistakable.

Far from being intimidated by the well-built, outgoing man who had approached her moments earlier, the pair were chatting and laughing as if they were old friends, which, of course, they probably were.

If I was to hazard a guess, I would say that Joseph Colmcille Savage had just told his customer a wicked anecdote, perhaps something to do with a deal he had done to get a special offer for the shop. Or he had confided some gossip about a local personality, which he had heard at second or

....

third hand and was passing on. And she was loving it, so much so that I feared for her health if he did not tone it down a bit!

It was a scene that was repeated time and again when you entered JC's supermarket in Swords, north County Dublin: JC, the owner of the shop, interacting with his 'audience', his customers, and making them feel special.

More often than not, the way he did this was by making them smile.

We visited JC's supermarket as part of the *Feargal Quinn's Retail Therapy* series. But, truth be told, it was a shop I knew only too well as Superquinn had opened a supermarket in Swords in 1986.

JC's was overseen by the late, great JC, who featured in the programme itself not long before sadly he passed away. From the very first day we opened our doors we were acutely conscious of just how brilliant a competitor and shopkeeper JC was. His shop was known throughout the area for its deals and bargains and for the charismatic personality of its founder.

JC's is the largest independent supermarket in the country, with over 2,500 square metres of retail space.

Like Standún, the shop is an institution in its local area. It has been trading on the Rathbeale Road since November 1977, although the family's roots in the area stretch back over 150 years.

Also like Standún, and many other family-run shops around the country, the company had a number of significant challenges when it came to charting its way out of the recession.

At the time of filming, JC was acutely aware of the need to plan for the future. There were a number of concerns facing the business he had so painstakingly built up over the years.

First, his family-run shop was facing increased competition from local rivals in a fiercely competitive marketplace. The arrival of low-cost retailers such as Aldi and Lidl in recent years was a significant additional pressure.

On top of this, supermarkets across the border in Northern Ireland were only an hour away, with an excellent motorway offering local customers easy access to their special offers. Sales at JC's, while healthy, were down 6 per cent. Wages were up 4 per cent.

Although JC's remained a very profitable business, it was clear it could not continue to trade on its founder's personality indefinitely.

Three of JC's sons, Michael, Niall and Robert, worked in management at the shop. Having access to these enthusiastic young men, eager to develop and safeguard the business for the future, should have been a huge plus for this family business.

Yet, when I asked them about their role in the shop, I was surprised to hear them respond almost identically: each said his role was to supervise the checkouts and ensure everything ran smoothly for the customer. One son, Niall, looked after ordering stock as well.

I was amazed to learn they had no specified managerial role in the supermarket. They lacked clearly defined responsibilities within the shop, an essential component in any healthy business looking to prepare itself for the future.

My concern was that JC was missing the opportunity to tap into his sons' enthusiasm and drive in a way that allowed them to show real initiative when it came to decision-making. Instead, I sensed all three were perhaps struggling to come out from behind the very long shadow cast by their hugely successful father.

To his credit, JC himself was conscious of the need to find a successor. But this was all very well in theory. In practice, I felt that maybe a part of him was reluctant to let go.

This did not surprise me unduly. Given my own business background, I know just how difficult this can be. How on earth do you plan for succession in a family-run business? And what are the pitfalls of failing to do so?

Well, the fact is that founders very rarely sack themselves. But sometimes they do step aside, when the time comes for a new generation to take over the business.

This in itself can be a tricky proposition: unless the handover is plotted carefully by all concerned it can be very tough for the founder to face up to a future where he or she is not part of the day-to-day decision-making process. This is particularly true when the founder is still involved in the company, perhaps as a figurehead, but is no longer the boss.

Equally, for the generation coming up behind the founder, it can be difficult to move forward on their own initiative without constantly doffing their caps to the instincts of their predecessor, particularly if the founder is still hanging around.

Yet it has always been my firm belief that in order to keep still in business you have to keep moving forward. If you want things to stay the same, namely the business to continue as a sound, profitable enterprise, then things have to continually change.

Like it or not, this includes laying the foundations that will allow your family-owned company, small business or corner shop to thrive *without* the person who first started it.

It became clear to me some years ago that we had to tackle this potentially thorny issue head-on at Superquinn. I knew I would not be with the business for ever, so we needed to plan for a future without Feargal Quinn at Superquinn. When you have spent the majority of your working life building up your company from scratch, this is never an easy thing to admit. Indeed, it can sometimes be difficult to avoid invoking the IOTFC rule, 'I Own The Company.' And we will do things My Way.

For Ever.

QED.

Its mischievous twin sister, of course, is the JFDI–IOTFC rule: Just Do It – I Own The Company!

Yet I also knew deep down that it was essential for our family business to make a proper plan for succession.

For many years, our elder children, Eamonn, Stephen and Gilliane, were involved in a variety of international organisations that specialised in addressing issues of concern to family-run businesses.

Stephen tells the story of attending one such family business conference at a prominent US university. The man leading the discussion asked how many present in the room were from first-generation businesses. Approximately 50 per cent put up their hand. When he asked how many were second-generation, around 30 per cent put up their hand.

Then he asked how many were third-generation, and 15 per cent put up their hand. By the time he reached fifth-generation businesses, and no hands were going up, he stopped and noted how unusual it is for companies to go beyond the third generation.

There is a reason for this. When it comes to succession, it can be incredibly difficult to ensure a smooth transition between the generations. All too often family businesses can end up shattering under the weight of competing agendas and familial rows, leading to immense damage for all concerned.

In any family business, there are a range of different drivers, because each of the people concerned comes from different perspectives. Perhaps there is someone with legal or financial expertise who married into the family and is telling his wife, 'You should be getting more of this, you should be getting more dividends. Look at your man there, he's getting a new car. Why are you not getting one too?'.

Meanwhile, management may want to take bigger risks so as to get bigger bonuses. Or the opposite may be true:

they may want to take a more conservative approach, 'We would like this business to move along nice and gently.'

Bearing all of this in mind, one of the greatest challenges to any family business is to decide who is the appropriate family member, or outsider, to oversee the future development of the company. At the same time, it is important to avoid in-fighting over who shares the financial spoils.

While there are many challenges particular to family-run businesses, it is not all doom and gloom.

As a family, we've had a close association with France for many years. My sister Eilagh had the opportunity to spend a year at school in Nantes in western France, and her husband, Jack McCabe, was the first Irish recipient of the honour of Chevalier du Tastevin (Brotherhood of the Knights of the Wine Tasting Cup).

It was a natural step to have our children spend some time in France before they were fourteen years old – the only problem was that the two girls, Gilliane and Zoë, both fell in love with Frenchmen at that age. In fact, they now both have French husbands – although not the boys they met when they were thirteen!

I later became Chairman of CIES, the worldwide retail organisation based in Paris.

Our family links with France enabled me to meet, and learn from, many French business families. More specifically, I saw how they faced up to the very particular challenges that a modern competitive market creates.

The Mulliez family provide a good example of how

One of the greatest challenges to any family business is to decide who is the appropriate family member, or outsider, to oversee the future development of the company to facilitate a healthy sense of entrepreneurship among the younger generations in a family-run business.

The clan owns and runs Groupe Auchan SA. They are one of the biggest international retail families in the world and have their headquarters in Croix, Nord-Pas-de-Calais. The company began when Gerard Mulliez opened his first self-service shop in Roubaix in the district of Hauts-Champs, which is pronounced the same as 'Auchan'.

Auchan started in 1961 and now has almost 2,000 shops with over a quarter of a million employees throughout the world.

They also happen to own Decathlon, a major chain of sports stores located around the world.

The story behind how Decathlon came into being is fascinating. Some time ago, *famille* Mulliez introduced a policy that said the family would help any member of the next generation who wanted to start a business. What they were saying was that they would trust the instincts of any of the family's next generation by supporting them in their plans, whatever they might be.

And it was this very policy that led one of the family members to start Decathlon.

The result? Auchan, one of the biggest supermarket companies in the world, is owned by the Mulliez family. Meanwhile, another completely independent and equally successful company, Decathlon, is also owned by the Mulliez family!

Clearly, in this instance family resources had been used to brilliant effect.

Another family-owned business that we interacted with and learned from over the years was the giant Publix company, based in Florida. Its founder, George Jenkins, started his supermarket empire in Winter Haven, Florida, in 1930.

His one shop has since grown to over 1,000 in Florida, Georgia, Alabama, South Carolina and Tennessee.

It's still a family-run business, and I have spent some time with members of the Jenkins clan in the USA.

Publix has a very well worked-out employee share profit scheme. It is owned by more than 96,000 stockholders and more than 113,000 participants of its Employee Stock Ownership Plan.

This makes it the largest employee-owned supermarket chain in the USA, with annual sales of more than $27 billion in 2011 alone.

This only happened because George Jenkins gave 85 per cent of the company's shares to its Employee Stock Ownership Plan. His heirs and other close colleagues control the rest.

The shares are currently traded privately and can be cashed in, usually when leaving the company, but only by selling them back to Publix.

When George decided to include the employees in this way, he explained, you should 'never be greedy with the employees who made you successful'.

'It motivates them to treat the customer like a king because it gives them some skin in the game', his grandson and current CEO Ed Crenshaw has since said.

Although the Jenkins family remains at the helm of the company, the introduction of this policy allowed employees and management to directly benefit from the growth and profitability of the chain. This is a hugely powerful motivator for the staff and says a lot about the culture of the company itself.

The John Lewis Partnership in the UK, in which the founder created an employee-owned co-operative, is another interesting example of how to reward the people who help make the business what it is.

Under this model, all 81,000 permanent staff at the firm are partners who own thirty-nine John Lewis shops across the UK, 288 Waitrose supermarkets and other related businesses. The partnership has annual gross sales of over £8.7 billion, so partners share in the benefits and profits of a business that puts them first.

Interestingly, when the co-operative's founder, John Spedan Lewis, set up the partnership, he was careful to create a governance system. This was formally set out in a constitution that would be democratic, giving every partner a voice in the business they co-own.

Each of the positive examples above has one thing in common: the fact that a *proactive* decision was taken within the company to discuss the future development of the business and the role that family members and employees would play, in a structured manner.

By so doing, they have cleverly steered their businesses away from many of the traditional pitfalls that can await inter-generational family enterprises.

I learned a lot about succession from these types of family businesses over the years. So much so that shortly after we celebrated Superquinn's fortieth birthday in 2000, I resolved to approach the question of succession in our business like they had: in as structured and rational a way as possible. In truth, this was the key to how we managed our family planning at Superquinn.

Rather than giving in to the temptation to view succession as a potential threat to my own role and legacy within Superquinn, it seemed pretty clear to me that the handover of the business to the next generation simply had to be planned properly. Otherwise, it had the potential to destabilise the entire company. I felt duty-bound to ensure this simply did not happen.

I have to say it helped enormously to treat the topic of succession planning just like we would any other major threat to our company. If Superquinn was to continue to thrive, then we needed to avoid the very real potential risks to its future that poor or inadequate family planning might create.

Removing my personal feelings from the equation, and calling a spade a spade, provided a real spur to action when it came to plotting a future for Superquinn *sans moi*.

And the way we resolved to address this issue was actually simple enough: we decided to HAVE THE CONVERSATION.

15

Have the conversation

*Don't let unspoken words threaten
the future of your business*

....

There is a reason why I put that phrase in block capitals at
the end of the last chapter, and why I have even given it a
brand spanking new chapter all of its own.

Although it may seem like a straightforward concept,
you would be amazed at how few family businesses ever get
so far as to acknowledge the need for the family-planning
conversation to take place.

Instead, they choose to let matters remain unspoken,
often with dire consequences for their businesses (and, in
some cases, their family relationships).

....

Simply ignoring the elephant in the room and hoping it goes away is not an option: if you ignore such a large animal in your home, it will invariably break all of your best china, and possibly much else besides.

The particular way we chose to HAVE THE CONVER-SATION (there I go again!) in our family was by writing our own Quinn Family Constitution.

This process involved getting our family together to discuss the vision and ethos of the company, as well as issues of succession, in an open and structured way.

First of all, each of our family members, and we have five children, took part in various courses on family business planning. Next, we set aside a number of days to work together on this specific issue. Nothing, and I mean nothing, was left off the table during this time.

We were fortunate to be able to bring in Tony Bogod, an expert in family business planning, as an outside adviser. Tony proved to be of real value in talking us through the process. Unlike many of those in the room, he also had the hugely beneficial virtue of being emotionally unattached to the outcome.

Among the many issues we examined were: What comes next? Who inherits the business? Do all of the children inherit it equally? Do they all run it equally? Or do we break it up and give everyone four shops and then tell them to go away? Or do you give it to the eldest son – which our eldest son, Eamonn, of course jokes he thought was a brilliant idea!

Did all of the children want to continue in the Superquinn business? Just because the business exists, it doesn't follow that this is what you want to do with your life. And how do you put a value on the company, if somebody does in fact want to exit?

By HAVING THE CONVERSATION, and asking ourselves the difficult questions outlined above, we were ultimately able to articulate our shared aims for the company in a clear and objective fashion. This turned out to be invaluable to us, both as a company and, far more importantly, as a family who happened to own a business together.

I actually have a copy of the Quinn Family Constitution on the table beside me as I write this. It is dated November 2002 and runs to over twenty pages with 8,000 words.

So what does it say? Well, first of all the document itself sets out 'the principles and practices' to be observed by the family shareholders.

Among the many practical issues it addresses are share ownership and dividends, including what happens if a member of the family wants to sell some or all of their shareholding; the composition and selection of the company's board of directors; and our overall corporate mission.

Yet the document does far more than simply address the major logistical considerations for our family business. Crucially, it also addresses our core values and our shared vision for our company in a way that we had never sat down and explicitly formulated before. This comes back to the whole idea of setting the tone (see Chapter 1) for what was, after all, our family company.

Elsewhere, the constitution contains a pretty forthright statement of our values. It says that, 'We, as a family, will endeavour to take pride in everything we do, to respect others, to act fairly and still maintain a sense of humour.'

As we have seen in previous chapters, the emphasis on humour was, we felt, a very important part of what made our company such a success (although some of my grandchildren will doubtless tell you how they groan at my 'bad jokes'!).

We also set the tone for our family company in another way by formulating our mission statement within our constitution. This was intended to act as a sort of blueprint or roadmap for the way ahead as we saw it, and it reads as follows: 'To be a world-class team renowned for excellence in fresh food and customer service.'

The document expands on the mission statement by noting how important it was to us that 'our behaviour as a family and a business must ensure that we continue to be highly respected.'

During our discussions, we also agreed it was important to include a section that outlined our family's vision for Superquinn in the future. We decided, after much deliberation, that this type of *vision statement* should include an explicit emphasis on the role our family culture would play in the development of the company.

We felt so strongly about this that the document specifically states our vision for the company was 'to see Superquinn successfully continue to grow, driven by its mission statement, whilst maintaining family culture and values. We consider family culture and values to be fundamental strengths of the business.'

In drawing up our constitution, we made a point of noting that not all family members would agree with every one of its provisions. However, we stressed that what had emerged from our discussions had been 'carefully thought out, discussed, written down and contained in an unambiguous document representing a consensus view'.

Again, this was hugely important as it allowed us to set out in black and white the exact terms and conditions under which our constitution had been developed, something that would help us to avoid any misunderstandings in the future.

Another important element of our constitution was a section that outlined our decision to set up a family council. The aim of this family advisory body was to help us discuss issues pertaining to the family's involvement in the company in a semi-formal, structured setting.

It comprised all members of the first (Denise and I) and second generation (our children), with provisions for subsequent generations to join the council. Again, there was a significant emphasis on a consensus-based approach.

In our document, we outlined some of the major issues for consideration by the family council. These included the appointment of family members to positions within Superquinn; offering guidance to members of the family on career opportunities and relevant qualifications either within or outside the family business; the development of a philanthropic fund; and the education of family members on family business issues generally.

We agreed that family-council meetings would be

convened approximately twice a year, with one such meeting followed by a wider family meeting once a year. This family meeting was to be principally a social occasion to which all spouses of the second generation would be invited, together with all children.

Importantly, we decided that the family council would also play a central role in advising on any proposed sale or closure of the company. Similarly, it was tasked with regularly assessing 'the contribution made to the business by its being family-owned and by the family culture, so as to satisfy them that these attributes continue to be a fundamental strength and a net advantage to the business.'

During our discussions leading up to the compilation of the Quinn Family Constitution, we formulated a de-facto succession plan for Superquinn. In public companies that are not doing well, the management typically gets sacked and new management is put in. In this way, the problem of under-performance is generally solved, for good or for bad.

But if a family-run business is not doing well, there can be a risk they will stick to the old way of doing things for too long rather than replacing the family member(s) in charge. A sometimes misplaced sense of family loyalty means that these businesses don't necessarily have the flexibility to bring in the right people to help them turn things around. Instead, they keep trying and trying until eventually they run the company or shop into the ground.

One of the important issues to emerge from our family brainstorming sessions was our agreement that the family business should exist to support the family, and not the other way around. At first glance, this might seem a pretty obvious statement. But the implications of this are quite profound for all family businesses, when you think about it. Basically we were agreeing that our priority was to look after the business first, which in turn would help the family, rather than doing things for the family and making the business suffer the consequences.

We felt so strongly about this issue that we inserted the following statement into our constitution, which is based on the concept of 'competence to the top': 'Entry into the business will be an opportunity, not a birthright, and high levels of commitment and performance will be expected from working family members.'

We went on to state that any family member who wished to apply for a permanent working position within Superquinn 'must first inform the family council. The council's decision as to whether the application should be permitted to proceed will be final.'

Similarly, we required that family members 'should be suitable, in terms of education, qualifications, character and experience for the posts available and should have held a position of authority within another organisation, unrelated by ownership, for a minimum of three years'.

There were a number of reasons why we chose to set out our thoughts on the above in such explicit terms within our own family constitution.

What we were getting at was that the business was there to provide for the family. But this didn't mean the family necessarily had to work in the business. Indeed, we also made a point of noting elsewhere in the constitution that as a family we recognised 'that individuals remain valued members of the family regardless of whether or not they have retained their shares'.

Clearly, if the business was not strong, then it would not be able to continue to provide for the family indefinitely. But to have a strong business we needed to have the best management. And if the best management weren't family, then they weren't family.

Thus, any family member at Superquinn had to be there on merit, rather than as a 'nod' to their family links. Of course this did not preclude family members from occupying senior roles in Superquinn. But where this happened they had to first prove their qualifications for the job. And they did.

It is my firm belief that any family-run business, no matter how large or small, should be just as willing to question its recruitment of family members in this way.

Why does the shop or business exist? Is it to provide employment for the family member who has taken over the day-to-day running of the business from the previous generation? If yes, is the person in question the best person to do this? Should consideration be given to bringing in outside expertise or to providing the family member with relevant training in their areas of weakness?

If the business does not necessarily exist to provide employment for the family, then might it be of more benefit

Mind Your Own Business

to hire other suitably qualified people to manage its development (with the family playing an advisory role)? Is this even financially possible, given the size and turnover of the business in question?

No two businesses will have the same answers. But the simple act of posing these types of questions in the first place will usually throw up some challenging, and ultimately exciting, responses. And, in my experience, in business this is very rarely a bad thing.

I found the process of drawing up our family constitution and mission statement absolutely fascinating, not least because I realised just how much we all agreed on our overall vision for the business. For example, we felt it was important the company would remain as a stand-alone business, even if it was not independent. Similarly, we wanted Superquinn, the brand, to survive if at all possible.

All of this careful planning and these new arrangements were put to the test more quickly than we might have imagined, and really proved their worth. A few years later, when business conditions generally were exceptionally buoyant and the company was in good health, we were very strongly advised to consider a sale of the business. The advice surprised us, but the setting up of the family council and the agreed procedures enabled us to HAVE THE CONVERSATION once again! And after much discussion and with some reluctance we accepted an offer from outside investors for the company.

There were several other advantages to our planned, structured approach to plotting for a future without me

Any family-run business, no matter how large or small, should be just as willing to question its recruitment of family members at Superquinn. First, as my son Eamonn points out, you can't really say over Sunday dinner, 'OK, so who is getting the business?'

But by formally planning a series of family meetings with this sole topic in mind, we were able to have exactly that conversation, warts and all. This also served to address any concerns among the younger generation that they might be seen to be wishing to elbow their elders out of the way in their lust for control.

Second, as mentioned above, we had already been thinking about these issues through the attendance at family business conferences. Having access to the viewpoints of other people facing similar issues, all over the world, certainly helped.

In any family business, there are certain issues that can be difficult to verbalise. But when everyone there is facing similar problems, this makes such conversations immeasurably easier.

Eamonn explains how the diversity in backgrounds of the people at these meetings was of real benefit. Some were second-generation family members and business managers while some didn't work in the business at all. There were doctors, lawyers, estate agents or dentists, and they were wondering what to do with the successful business or practice they had built up.

In many cases, the businesses were ticking away quite nicely. But the family members who had inherited them, or who were due to inherit them, didn't know what to do next. If they were non-executives, sometimes they had come to the realisation that they weren't competent to make a decision. But if this is the case, who do you appoint to do it for you?

Our two eldest children, Eamonn and Gilliane, attended one family business meeting at the IMD business school in Lausanne, Switzerland. I remember well their bubbly enthusiasm when they came home, all excited about the 'How to Get Rid of the Founder' session, although the actual title was the more polite 'How a Founder May Exit the Family Business'.

'There are four different types of founder,' Gilliane explained. 'The first is the Emperor who never retires – he dies on the job.'

'The second is the General,' said Eamonn. 'He hands the running of the business to his successor, saying, "I'm off into the sunset. Best of luck lads, you take care of everything." But he comes back a year later with the words, "Gosh, you are making an awful mess of things" and takes over the reins again.'

'The one I like is the Ambassador,' continued Gilliane. 'He becomes chairman of a bank, or gets himself elected a Senator! So he eases himself out of the business, is available for advice, but doesn't interfere.'

The fourth example they did not like at all. The Philanthropist simply gives it all away!

JC's supermarket in Swords, Co. Dublin, is an excellent example of the issues facing thousands of family businesses the world over. While the supermarket is far larger than most family-owned corner shops or butcher's shops, the principle that made it such a success remain the same: personality.

But the very thing that made JC Savage's company stand out also left it with a significant challenge: how to ensure the shop would continue to thrive during a major economic downturn when JC was no longer around to steer it.

Eventually, JC addressed this by allocating specific roles to each of his sons within the shop. Each is a director of the company. Robert is primarily responsible for the shop floor and checkouts. Niall runs the storeroom and shop floor with Robert, while Michael, as Managing Director, takes overall responsibility for the business. Meanwhile, the family holds regular family business meetings that are attended by their mother Geraldine too. These were all the types of positive changes JC and I had discussed during my time at the shop.

And I am glad to say that JC's sons have risen with aplomb to the task of filling the huge void left by their father's untimely death. I can offer no higher praise than to say that the supermarket remains a thorn in the side of its many competitors in Swords and beyond.

During a recent visit to the shop, I was also glad to see that JC's lifelong emphasis on pleasing the customer is still to the forefront in all the shop does.

I have no doubt he is smiling down from above with immense pride at the legacy he has left behind.

16

Why Bono is right

Sometimes you can't make it on your own — learn to stand on the shoulders of others

....

Some years ago, Tony Donnelly approached me with an unusual proposition. I had known Tony for years. He had previously worked with Fyffes, a major fruit supplier, and had set up his own fruit-supply business under the name Anthony Donnelly Ltd.

Tony asked me, 'Would you guarantee me your fruit and vegetable business for the next year? You see, if I knew I had all of your business, I could visit Spain and visit Italy and visit France, and I would buy the grapes, I would buy the

....

oranges, I would order them in advance, and I would get the best quality. I would know they were the best price because I would be buying for the whole year.

'But I couldn't do that unless I knew I had your business. If I had it, I would be willing to show you my invoices, show you what I am paying, how much profit I am making. And you would know you were getting the best price and the best quality and the best flavour and the best freshness possible because you trust me to buy in advance.'

You see, up until that point, every Friday at Superquinn we would go to the six or so biggest fruit importers and say, 'Give us a quote for bananas, oranges, grapes', and whatever other fruit and vegetables were going to be imported that week.

They would give us their samples and prices. Then, on Saturday morning, we would give the successful supplier the order for the following week.

Our aim in doing this was to ensure we got the best quality and value possible from our fresh-fruit suppliers every week.

I could see the logic to Tony's proposal. If we could maintain a viable, long-term relationship with his company, we could use his expertise to ensure we had access to the very best fruit and vegetables on offer.

But in order to do this, I had to place my complete trust in Tony to deliver for Superquinn. I mulled it over for some time before deciding to take a leap of faith with Tony. It was a big decision for our company.

I told him, 'OK, Tony, I trust you to do a good job for us, so go ahead. You have my word that we will take our imported fruit exclusively from you for the next year.'

Shortly afterwards, we closed our accounts with the other five companies, who, of course, were not happy at all to be losing our custom.

But even when these other suppliers approached us looking to beat Tony's price – in some cases even by selling below cost – I turned them down flat. 'No, I trust Tony,' was my standard reply.

More than twenty-five years later, Superquinn is still dealing with Tony Donnelly's family company. What's more, because of our extremely close working relationship, his company played a major role in helping our shops provide the best quality fruit around, bar none.

The reason I tell this story is to illustrate one of the great positives of business life. As the old saying goes, no man is an island. But it is just as true that no business is an island, either.

Whether we realise it or not, every business operates as part of a wider community. Other local businesses, trade associations, trusted suppliers, customers and the banks are just some of those who form part of this shared community.

During a recession, when budgets are particularly tight, every business needs to learn how to utilise these resources to their full effect; they need to learn that even when times are tough, they are not alone.

My father had a golden rule in business, which was you should never give your banker any surprises.

Whether we realise it or not, every business operates as part of a wider community

What he meant by this was that you should always give your banker an honest picture of where you are financially.

His logic was that by being upfront and honest in this way you were putting your trust in your bank. In turn, they would support you if and when times were tough, or indeed if you needed finance to expand your business.

From my earliest days as a retailer, I sought to cultivate my relationships with my suppliers, with people like Tony Donnelly as a priority (as well as with my bankers!).

Often, I found the sheer strength of these relationships pushed us all to excel in ways that others would have never thought possible.

Let me give you an example.

Some years ago, we asked ourselves at Superquinn, 'How can we have an advantage over Tesco?'

The answer was, 'If we could manage to say that our products are fresher than theirs.'

We went to the late Brian Donnelly, Tony's son, and asked him to approach his growers to ask, 'Is it possible that the cabbage on our shelves could only be today's cabbage, cut today? Could we put the date and a signature from you on it saying, "This cabbage was cut today, Tuesday, 11 August at 6 a.m."?'

We were wondering if it was logistically possible for Brian to get the produce into our shops before we opened at 9 a.m.

Now, we knew well this was a big 'ask'. What we wanted was for Superquinn to be the only supermarket in Ireland that offered its customers cabbage or cauliflower or leeks that had been harvested only a few hours earlier.

Often, I found the sheer strength of these relationships pushed us all to excel in ways that others would have never thought possible

We were aware there was no way that larger shops such as Tesco and Marks and Spencer, who were probably getting their fresh vegetables delivered by truck overnight, could compete with that, given their size.

There was nothing really wrong with their produce. But it was probably a few days old, and it would have been chilled during delivery. Our aim was for Superquinn customers to be able to buy vegetables that were cut just a few hours earlier.

By setting the bar so high, I was deliberately laying down a challenge to one of our most trusted suppliers. He knew I wanted him to deliver.

'Could you do that?' we asked Brian.

'Yes, we could do it during the summer because it's bright enough to be able to cut it. We could get up at 5 a.m. or 6 a.m. and cut the cabbage. But we couldn't do it during the winter when it's dark,' Brian responded.

'OK. Well, we might have to find somebody else who can, because I want to be able to say, "We only sell vegetables that are cut today", I responded, upping the ante.

'Jeepers, you can't do that. Look at this field, and that

field, they are all growing for you. You can't, you can't not take them –'

'Yes, but our standard now is today's vegetables cut today!'

It was then that Brian's son, Ciaran, said, 'Do you know what we could do? If we put miner's lamps on our foreheads, we could actually cut them in the dark at 5 a.m. or 6 a.m. when it's dark in the winter.'

And they ended up doing just that, except instead of using miner's lamps they used tractor lights.

Never being one to miss an opportunity to show just how nimble we were as a business, we went on to display photographs in our shops of them out picking the vegetables in the dark.

I don't think I could have pushed Brian Donnelly to deliver for me as he did unless I had cultivated such a close working relationship with him and his father previously.

Out of a sense of loyalty to our company, Brian's growers strove to stretch the boundaries of what was perceived as being possible in the most wonderful way.

The benefits of this to my company were enormous as it allowed us to differentiate ourselves from our larger competitors. In turn, Brian had the benefit of knowing Superquinn valued him as a trusted supplier.

I have previously outlined examples of where I saw other businesses around the world doing things that we then 'borrowed' for our shops. Frequently, these innovations – such as in-store bakeries and sausage-making plants – went on to become synonymous with the Superquinn brand.

The only reason we were able to innovate in this way was because we realised just how important it was to learn from others, including our competitors.

The truth is that every small business should be willing to stand on the shoulders of others, if they are really serious about excelling in their chosen field. Let me give you another example of how we did this at Superquinn.

Loyalty cards are commonplace in supermarkets nowadays. But in 1993, Superquinn was the first supermarket in Europe to introduce the idea of these cards.

The way it worked was that customers earned a Super-Club point for every £1 they spent. They could then exchange these points for any of more than 200 gifts in our SuperClub catalogue.

The whole concept of a customer loyalty card tied in perfectly with my belief in the need to reward our loyal customers properly.

But guess what?

I actually got the idea from British Airways, which had a long-standing air-miles loyalty scheme in place. I had also seen a similar system in operation in some stores in the USA.

Shortly after we introduced SuperClub, the heads of Tesco and Sainsbury's, both of which now run very elaborate customer loyalty schemes, came to visit Superquinn to see how our loyalty-club system worked. And I happily showed them around!

At the time, neither were direct competitors of ours in the Irish marketplace. I knew they would reciprocate if

Every small business should be willing to stand on the shoulders of others, if they are really serious about excelling in their chosen field

ever I wanted to see how they did things in their shops.

And they did.

One of the best examples from the television series of how to learn from others occurred when we worked with Denis Murphy at the BMC shop in Cobh.

As you will recall when we talked about him in Chapter 13, Denis had inherited his business from his father and his grandfather before him. At times, Denis struggled to overcome the hand of this history weighing on his shoulders.

But the good news was the huge tourist potential in BMC, Denis's shop. Its location on Cobh's main promenade meant that the shop was in an ideal situation to benefit from the thousands of cruise-ship visitors and crew and from the other tourists to this very popular port town.

However, it was being let down by its delicatessen counter, which should have been a significant income-generator for the business. When we visited, food prepared that morning had been sitting under heat lamps for some time, meaning that it did not look inviting.

I knew that if he could make a real success of the deli, Denis would bring people into the shop and could sell them other things too. It seemed clear to me that either he needed to do his deli very well, or not at all.

We took Denis and his colleague Faz to the Ardkeen Quality Food Store in Waterford. It was time for him to see how things should be done at a top-class deli counter and food store.

Located inside the bright, clean, well-laid-out shop, Ardkeen's deli counter was a joy to behold. You could almost taste the food as soon as you saw it, it was that good! We saw attentive, knowledgeable staff wearing branded uniforms and hats and could smell the aroma of fresh bread wafting through the shop.

Denis came away from this a man inspired.

Together we hatched a big plan to redesign BMC, and in particular its deli counter, to bring it up to date with modern retailing standards.

When the time came to relaunch BMC, to coincide with the arrival of the massive *Queen Mary 2* cruise liner into Cobh, Denis sent his staff out with samples of their new, tasty, fresh deli food to lure its thousands of passengers and crew inside.

And it worked brilliantly!

Because Denis had taken the time to study what his competitors were doing, and to learn from them, for the first time in years he knew exactly what was needed to chart the way forward for his shop.

This in turn prompted him to sanction the necessary investment to hugely improve his own deli counter and the food it offered. Banished for good were the Cornish pasties and breakfast baps, to be replaced with fresh, wholesome and inviting wraps and salads.

During our visit to Ardkeen, I asked Denis, 'What would happen if this shop was next door to you? How would you get customers to walk past this shop to come to you?'

The answer, as Denis soon saw, was that he needed to be at least as good as they were, if not better.

And he could do this only by being willing to stand on the shoulders of others, and to learn from them.

Clearly no business is an island. So it unfortunately came as little surprise to me that the Village Hardware Store in Rathfarnham was struggling badly when we visited it as part of the *Retail Therapy* series.

Brothers Patrick and Tony Quinlan opened their brand-spanking-new shop in June 2009.

Patrick is a trained civil engineer and Tony is a painter-decorator. Both had lived in Rathfarnham all their lives and believed the village was crying out for a hardware store.

The shop itself specialised in paint and in mixing colours as well as selling the standard hardware items. They also cut keys and offered a limited range of cookware.

But the brothers admitted they had absolutely no retail experience. They were at a loss as to how to make the business succeed and knew they desperately needed to establish a customer base in the locality.

They were not taking a wage from the business despite working six days a week, and any money they made was put back into the shop. As a result, they were living 'week to week' when we caught up with them for the first time.

Everything was on the line. As Patrick told the cameras, 'We don't have an option. We need to make this work.'

One of my big concerns with the Village Hardware Store was my sense that Patrick and Tony had not really thought things through before opening their doors.

From the outset, I was worried that the Quinlans had done little or nothing to tell people in their community they were open and available for business. They had failed to market their shop effectively in the locality.

Just as we saw with Caroline in Carrie's Cakes, it was as if they thought it was enough to throw all their energy into opening their doors and that trade would then follow. As their takings showed, it clearly was not working.

It also seemed they thought that just because they had built a 'mousetrap', people would beat a path to their door. You have to get customers to tell their friends about the existence of the mousetrap in the first place.

The Quinlans urgently needed to focus on getting new customers who in turn could become missionaries for their business.

Put simply, they needed a business plan. This would chart things such as what percentage their current sales were to the business market and how much to the DIY/ home-improvement market, and also how much selling they were doing to individuals coming in off the street.

Setting themselves growth targets for each of these markets would allow them to proactively develop their business in a planned, structured way. Indeed, there were grounds to believe that a constantly evolving business plan would pay real dividends.

We worked out that if they could manage to get even an extra four to six local painters to source their paint from them they could double their sales of paint instantly. However, I met a painter on the street a few metres from their door who didn't even know their shop was open in Rathfarnham!

It soon became clear that this was another of the brothers' big problems: they simply did not know how to attract customers or how to get them coming back in true boomerang style.

Inside the shop, there was little sense of excitement, with poor signage and inadequate promotion of their merchandise.

When we sent a secret shopper in, she was not enthusiastic about the reception she received or by the half-hearted attempt at upselling, which simply did not work.

It seemed as if they were sitting in their shop, saying, 'Oh, we want more business coming in.' This gave her a completely different message than intended. It screamed at her, 'This is our cave. Once we turn up every day and we are in our cave, then we are doing enough to get by.'

What they *should* have been doing, of course, was imagining that every person who came through their door was an influential critic who would be doing a mental report card on their shop.

This would have prompted them to realise that this person needed to be wowed by what they saw.

We knew we had to address their weaknesses in this regard – and fast! Patrick and Tony needed to start practising their sales techniques on real live customers.

We arranged a little experiment. We took them out to a local housing estate and asked them to go door to door, talking to local householders about what they needed from their village hardware store.

Both men were very nervous about doing this at first, even though they owned and operated a retail outlet! But, with time, they gained more confidence from the experience.

Again, this was something we were well used to doing in Superquinn, whenever we felt our colleagues needed help to boost their confidence. I remember one time in particular. Martin McArdle, manager in Superquinn Blanchardstown, had a very good assistant manager, Adrian Doyle.

Unfortunately, like many people, Adrian was rather shy, which Martin knew was holding him back on the shop floor.

So Martin brought Adrian to Grafton Street and asked him to walk from the bottom all the way up to the top, saying hello to every single person walking towards him.

And he did!

'Hello, hello, how are you?' he said as he made his way up Dublin's best known shopping street.

I'm sure Adrian got all sorts of looks as he did this. But to this day he considers it one of the most important lessons he learned. Many customers coming into his supermarket, Doyle's Eurospar, in Meakstown in Finglas, comment on how great it is to be welcomed into the shop, and they say to him that it seldom happens elsewhere. But, as with Patrick and Tony calling from door to door, Adrian very quickly got into the habit of being able to say hello to people.

Patrick and Tony did not know it, but there was another way for them to grow their business and also to benefit from the experience of others. They were not alone.

One of the most successful hardware groups in Ireland is Expert Hardware. Expert is a group of independent DIY merchants who come together to pool their expertise and to provide support to their fellow traders.

By joining them, Rathfarnham Village Hardware became a member of a group with real buying power.

This brought with it an obvious benefit: the ability to attract a better range of leading products such as Dulux paints, while at the same time being price-competitive when compared with the major multiples.

But there was another, arguably more important, advantage to getting involved with Expert. By joining the group, they had instant access to the support and advice of hundreds of other DIY merchants around the country, merchants who had been there, done that and bought the T-shirt.

Where before Patrick and Tony were sole traders battling (largely unsuccessfully) against the recession, this new sense of community helped them feel less alone in the marketplace.

When times are tough, this can be a huge source of comfort and support.

The commitment to no longer do things on their own did not stop there for the Quinlans. During the show we organised a group meeting of the businesses in Rathfarnham village, to look at ways of enticing more people to the area.

Instead of the brothers asking what they could do individually, we resolved to pose the simple question, 'What can you do together, as a business community that does not operate in a vacuum?'

The goodwill this generated was fantastic and culminated with the holding of an inaugural village fair. One local businessman said this was the first such festival in 200 years in the village!

The meeting led to plans for the construction of a new Rathfarnham Village website, where visitors could find details of all the local businesses under one online roof for the first time.

The coming together of local businesses to help each other chart the way out of recession is hugely valuable. It amazes me why others don't do it.

Instead of waiting around for someone else to do it for them, by developing their local resources all businesses can harness this energy in a fantastically positive way.

Since the show was broadcast, Patrick and Tony have decided to move away from the hardware business and have shut down their shop. Despite the initial upturn in business brought about from their participation in the show, they ultimately realised that the shop simply did not have a long-term future in that particular location.

All is by no means lost, however. Tony continues to run a very successful painting and decorating business, Arco Decor, and Patrick works with him too. Business is going well, and many of the lessons they learned from participating in the television programme have stood to them in this venture.

One of the most notable of these is the importance of utilising the local business community to generate trade and to support your enterprise.

U2's lead singer, Bono, had it right, you know: sometimes you can't make it on your own.

But no business should really have to either.

17

Small can be beautiful

*Become a master craftsman
at whatever you do*

....

The senior Sainsbury's executive was standing still, listening to me intently. During a tour of one of our Superquinn shops, we happened upon the stand containing our fresh orange juice, which we produced ourselves in-store every morning. At Superquinn, our policy was to only produce enough juice to sell on the day it was made, so it was always 100 per cent fresh. To reinforce this message to our customers, the label on the small carton of orange juice said, 'Squeezed Today', with the day and the date printed next to it. For example, 'Friday, 12 September'.

....

In fact, we had only started using that exact wording on our labels a short time before, after our supervisor in the fruit and vegetable department in Superquinn Carlow was approached by a customer. The customer explained, 'I buy the juice and put it in the fridge. I know it's fine for a few days, and then I open the fridge and I see "12 September". But I can never remember what the date is today. Is there any way you can put the day as well as the date on the label? This would make it much easier to know the quality of the juice I have in my fridge.'

He was right, of course. So, pretty much the next day, the manager in Superquinn Carlow changed the labels on our fresh juices to state clearly, 'Friday, 12 September' – or whatever the day was. Within three days, we had changed the labels in all of our Superquinn shops to reflect this customer's wish. This was because his comments had been passed up the management chain quickly and we had adjusted our labelling machines easily.

I told this story, almost as an aside, to the Sainsbury's executive, as we stood looking at the orange-juice display. I found his reply fascinating: 'You know, if that happened in our company it would take at least six months to get that done. We have so many controls and systems that we couldn't do that in one week.'

This brought home to me the fact that in business size is not everything. Sometimes there are major advantages to being smaller than your competitors: it allows you to be different. What's more, it allows you to be nimble, too.

As the owners of a 140-square-metre pet shop trading from the Village Green in Tallaght, Dublin 24, husband-and-wife team Des and Marion Scanlon were only too aware of the challenges that larger rivals posed to their business. The Tallaght Pet Shop had been open for eighteen years and had extended its floor size significantly over that time.

The shop employed two full-time staff members, in addition to the owners, and it was feeling the brunt of the recession badly. Many of its biggest-spending customers during the 'boom' years had been foreign nationals who had either gone home since the economy collapsed or were no longer spending on their pets as they used to do.

Yet Des told me that the shop also had a loyal customer base that would drive past other pet shops just to go to them. Business had been good until relatively recently. But, with sales dropping, both Des and Marion were desperate to keep the shop trading.

The shop's problems did not end there. When we first visited, it was packed to the rafters with stock accumulated over the past eighteen years. It was in need of a serious decluttering to make the customer's experience easier. It also needed to change its layout to get away from the 'pile 'em high' look.

As with the McGreal's and Burgess Department Stores mentioned in Chapters 4 and 7, the Tallaght Pet Shop had an image problem that began with its front-of-store display. Instead of displaying their wares properly outside on the pavement, Des and Marion had lined up lots of dog kennels

> Sometimes there are major advantages to being smaller than your competitor: it allows you to be different. What's more, it allows you to be nimble, too.

in front of their shop window, virtually obscuring the rest of the shop. This gave passers-by the false impression that they were primarily in the dog-kennel business, rather than being a pet shop that sold twenty varieties of bird, guinea pig, rabbit, hamster, parrot, fish, snake, lizard, tarantula, turtle, terrapin and tortoise, as well as pet food (frozen mice and rats, crickets, locusts, etc.) and all types of pet accessories. When a crocodile line of schoolchildren walked past the pet-shop window without one of them stopping to see what cute animals were inside, we knew something was seriously wrong.

Yet another major and pressing concern was the proliferation of pet superstores that had popped up around Dublin during the boom years. Two such shops were both located within a short drive of the pet shop, offering a range of goods with which the Tallaght Pet Shop simply could not compete. Or could it?

One of the very first things we did when we began to work with Des and Marion was to visit the nearby MaxiZoo Superstore, alternatively known as Their Major Competitor. It is an Irish-owned franchise of a huge German multinational chain. Now, MaxiZoo is a very well run business with knowledgeable staff. It is an efficient shop, with rows upon rows of well-laid-out pet accessories. But, due to its sheer size, I felt it lacked the charisma of the Tallaght Pet Shop.

The truth is that Des and Marion became involved in the pet-shop business out of their passion for animals. Both of them loved the idea of having their own shop, because they loved animals and wanted to work with them. They also wanted to be able to pass on their expertise to fellow animal lovers, by advising them how best to care for their pets. Owning and running their own shop was almost a vocation for them. 'We put our hands in the weirdest of places here. We clean up the weirdest things here' was how Des described it to me at one stage.

I knew we needed to find a way to get this passion across to prospective customers, by trading on the individuality of this smaller, specialist shop.

Throughout my time at Superquinn we were faced with challenges similar to those of the Tallaght Pet Shop. As a comparatively small, yet high-quality player in the Irish supermarket business, we realised from an early stage just how important it was to emphasise what made us different from our much larger competitors.

More often than not the way we did this was by deliberately trading on our personality, in order to stand out from the crowd. One key way of doing this was by developing a sustained media presence. This was something I undertook personally by always making myself available for comment.

In the early days of Superquinn, we had only one shop in Dublin, and I read the paper each morning to see what was topical. Then I would pick up the phone to the *Evening Herald*. 'Could I talk to a reporter about this story? Who's handling the one about the half-crown being abolished?', or whatever the story of the day was. You see, I had learned very early on that the afternoon papers, such as the *Evening Herald*, the *Evening Press* and the *Evening Mail*, would go to press at about 10 a.m. There were editors and reporters in there scratching their heads saying, 'What will I put in the paper today?' If they got a supermarket in Finglas complaining about the suggestion that the half-crown be abolished or the farthing be abolished, or something else you could find from the news of the day, they would mention the supermarket in the paper. This was a brilliantly simple form of free advertising.

Not all of the publicity we generated for our shop was entirely positive. In the 1960s, we gave a free goldfish in a bag for every half pound of Hughes silver-label tea you bought. I really shouldn't be telling you this ... but we then arranged for somebody to write to the *Evening Press* to complain about a supermarket giving out free live goldfish. In turn, they carried the story where somebody said they thought it was outrageous that this supermarket in Dundalk was giving a free goldfish with every half-pound of silver-label tea. However, we were delighted, as, despite the controversy, we knew it made us different to the bigger players in the minds of our customers.

I didn't even know the expression 'PR' at the time. All I knew was that over and over again people would come across the name and say, 'Oh, that's the supermarket in Dundalk I read about the other day.' It was a very cost-effective type of 'guerrilla' marketing for our small shop.

During a recession, every business person should be looking to establish a link with their local papers and local radio stations. With the advent of the Internet, the scope for smaller businesses to trade on their personality in this way is arguably even greater than ever.

The Tallaght Pet Shop had a trump card when it came to generating PR for their shop: Des and Marion's passion for what they did. We just needed to find a way to get the message across that anyone coming to their shop was dealing with individuals who were real personalities. To coincide with the planned relaunch of the shop, we sent Des and Marion into the offices of the local newspaper, the *Tallaght Echo*, to tell them about the event.

They were clearly impressed and promised to send a reporter and photographer to cover the launch. We organised a photo shoot featuring Des and Marion alongside some of the animals from their shop. You can imagine their surprise when we showed them an image of themselves blown up on a giant mobile billboard for all to see! Again, this tied in perfectly with our master plan to use the personalities of the Tallaght Pet Shop's owners to separate it from its larger competitors.

Des and Marion needed another angle to coax pet owners from the Tallaght area into the shop. Together they came up with the idea of installing a grooming parlour in the shop. The thinking behind this was to make the Tallaght Pet Shop the destination for pet-lovers who wanted to have their animal groomed. There were several notices up in the shop already from pet groomers, advertising their businesses, so this suggested to us that the demand was certainly there. The beauty of this was that once pet owners were inside the revamped shop we were confident that Des, Marion and their team would wow them with their knowledge and enthusiasm. This was something they had in bundles. We were sure that when these animal lovers got to know the team who worked there personally, in future they would be likely to get their pet accessories from them too.

This combination of personality, passion and knowledge, which Des and Marion had in spades, is a huge bonus for any small business during a recession. I would go so far as to say it is a secret weapon in the battle to stay afloat.

I was in Drogheda a while back, and at one stage I had to go back to the car to put money in the parking meter. I walked a different route back just to see and get a feel for the town. As I walked around, the one thing I came away with was how few small, specialist shops there are there. This worried me because discovering a specialist shop is like finding a hidden treasure. For example, if you go into a cobbler and they really educate you about the shoe you are wearing and how they will go about fixing it, you know you are in the presence of a master craftsman.

To be a master craftsman, like a cobbler, or butcher, or tailor, you not only need to know your trade inside out but you need to have a real passion for it, too. In Superquinn, we knew all about the benefits of having master craftsmen in our shops. This was one of the reasons we sent all of our butchers to cookery school. When they finished the course, they took great pride – rightly – in the fact that they knew how to cook. So they would regularly give customers advice.

One day I met a customer in Swords who told me she lived between Balbriggan and Drogheda and used to always shop in her local butcher's close to her home. But she happened to be in Dublin one day, and on her way home she realised, 'Oh, look at the time, I won't have time to do my shopping.'

She called in to Superquinn Swords, and as she came to the butcher's counter and looked at the meat, trying to decide what to buy, Trevor behind the counter said, 'What can I get you?'

She replied, 'I'll have that piece there,' pointing out some beef.

Then Trevor asked her, 'What are you going to do with it? Did you ever think of doing it this way?' before describing how to make a lovely dish with the meat she was buying. 'Oh, and open a bottle of wine. I would suggest a burgundy – and take a glass before you sit down!' he added.

In other words, he was telling her, 'I love my meat so much that I'm not going to give it to you unless you tell me what you will do!'

'Ever since then I won't shop anywhere else, except with Trevor, because no butcher ever looked after me that way,' she told me. 'I drive all the way from Drogheda, or wherever I am, to buy my meat from Trevor.'

Just like Trevor, I believe it is possible for a small business owner to be a master craftsman (or woman) at almost

> To be a master craftsman, like a cobbler, or butcher, or tailor, you not only need to know your trade inside out but you need to have a real passion for it, too.

anything. For example, as a small, specialist shop, I wanted Des and Marion to become master craftsmen in their chosen trade: pets.

All small businesses, whether they are a corner shop or an office supplies' business, can benefit from asking themselves, 'How do I become a master craftsman at what I do?' If you can focus on doing at least one thing brilliantly, this gives you a huge competitive advantage over your larger rivals. This is all the more true when you factor in the winning personalities of the people behind your company too.

Another way of looking at this is if you do not try to mark yourself out from your better resourced competitors, then you are just the same as everybody else. And if you are going to be the same as everybody else, people will say, 'I may as well go to the one nearest to me, or I may as well go to the one that's cheapest. There's no reason for me to make the effort to go elsewhere.'

Not every business owner wants to be the next Tesco, Walmart or Microsoft either. I firmly believe that being and remaining small is a very legitimate goal in itself, not least during a recession.

Sometimes this message that small can be beautiful gets drowned out in the rush to expand. When I first started out in business, my father asked me, as I prepared to open my third shop, 'What do you want to do? What do you want to be?' And I said, 'My mission is to be the best at food in Dublin.'

> If you can focus on doing at least one thing brilliantly, this gives you a huge competitive advantage over your larger rivals.

There was no mention that I wanted to have 150 shops. Also, there was no mention that I wanted to own the biggest chain of supermarkets in Ireland. And, although I did consider significantly expanding Superquinn on several occasions — for example by moving north of the border, ultimately I decided this was not what I wanted for my company.

This was because my goals were simple: I wanted to be the best at food in Dublin (and later in the south-east region). Also, I wanted to ensure I had a sustainable business model that suited this ambition. To do this, I felt it was more important for Superquinn to stay a manageable size than it was for it to overextend itself by expanding too much.

Many small businesses take a different approach, and some do so wrongly, in my view. Once they find a business model that is working, they almost immediately ask themselves, 'How can I franchise this and open up a lot more of these shops?' Sometimes they feel the only way to insulate themselves financially is to expand. Similarly, they might have investors who are aggressively looking to grow the business, and the profit margins. But this is not the same as creating a sustainable, viable business for the long term. As the recent recession has shown us, it is also far from ideal in the face of a volatile business climate. This is yet another reason why small can be beautiful. In business, there should always be room for the person who says, 'I want to be the best at food in Dublin.' Because it is OK to have an ambition other than to simply expand.

The legendary US retailer, Stew Leonard, about whom I spoke in Chapter 9, did not expand beyond his one dairy store for more than forty years, until one of his relatives opened a couple of new stores. While the store grew in size on its original site, he said, 'I don't see expansion as the be-all and end-all. I'm going to do a great job, I'm going to be famous for what I'm doing, and I'm going to do the one job.' Stew was confident about setting his own goals and following them during his business career. This led him to enjoy great, and enduring, success.

I have to say, I thought Stew was right to follow his own path rather than simply giving in to the pressure of endless expansion. There are businesses that sometimes think, 'Oh, I should be expanding, it's expected of me, that's what you do in business.' But rather than automatically saying, 'I've got this urgent need to expand,' sometimes it is better to say, 'I've got this urgent need not to expand. I need to ensure I am the best at what I do, and to do that, I need to stay small . . . at least for now.'

Because, in business, sometimes when everyone else is running, maybe that's the time for you to walk. And when everyone is walking, maybe that's the time for you to run. Or even just to jog on the spot, without ever losing your enthusiasm.

Epilogue

The date 25 November 1960 remains forever etched in my memory. It was a dull, slightly overcast day, with little to recommend it from a weather perspective at least. Yet, despite the rather dreary weather, I simply could not wait to get down to Clanbrassil Street in Dundalk that same morning. I was preparing to open my very first shop, Quinn's Supermarket, in the northern border town, and was absolutely brimming with enthusiasm.

I did not know it then, but as I pulled the shutters up on my first day, I was embarking on a lifelong love affair with retailing.

Almost half a century later, as I prepared to sell the company that bore my name, I could not help thinking back to that day. I remembered the enthusiastic young man who could barely sleep with excitement the night before our big opening. And I smiled to myself at the thought of how little has changed in the intervening years.

It is never an easy decision to sell the business you have established and run for forty-five years. This is true even when you are convinced it is in the best long-term interests of the company – and all of the stakeholders involved.

The truth is that very few large family businesses last beyond the third or fourth generation. Those that do have to be well geared for the challenges ahead.

One of the great privileges of my involvement in the *Feargal Quinn's Retail Therapy* television series has been the opportunity it provided for me to jump the retail counter once again and to go back to my roots as a grocer and retailer. It has been some journey.

Along the way, I met businesses run by women, men, husband-and-wife teams, fathers and sons, and fathers and daughters. It is fair to say that pretty much all walks of business life were represented in the case studies selected for the show.

As we have seen, every individual shop was also unique, in its own way. This is because the personalities, hopes and dreams of the people who worked there were each very different.

Yet at their core, all of them were seeking the same or similar things: practical tips and advice on how to adapt their businesses to serve their customers better. In turn this would allow them to plan for a future filled with confidence.

That is where this book comes in. My sincere hope is that the stories and lessons it contains have proved useful to you, during these tough economic times.

I would also like to think that by focusing on the positives that a recession can throw up this book will help ignite (or reignite!) a passion for business excellence in all who read it.

And if you can have lots of fun along the way, even better. Because I, for one, most certainly did!

Acknowledgements

There is an(other) old African proverb, which says, 'It takes a village to raise a child.' Well, I think the same can be said about writing a book.

In fact, when I first thought about writing *Mind Your Own Business* (as it has become), I asked myself three key questions.

The first of these was, 'Do I have enough current material that is relevant to the topics I want to explore?'

I have been truly fortunate to find, in the staff of Animo Productions and their colleagues at the Irish national broadcaster, RTÉ, a group of talented professionals committed to producing the *Feargal Quinn's Retail Therapy* series. Much of their work is reflected in the stories contained in this book, for which I am very thankful.

Second, I asked myself, 'Do I have a publisher who will have faith in this project and who will help me bring it to fruition?' This is where Michael O'Brien and all of his team in The O'Brien Press once again came to the fore. Not only did they believe in this book from the very start, they also put me in contact with Liz Hudson, the editor who wielded her 'little red pen' with style.

Third, I asked, 'Do I have a group of trusted friends and colleagues who can provide me with constructive criticism and helpful feedback?' Again, I have been so very lucky in this regard.

Put quite simply, this book would not exist without the help and support – and sometimes firm nudge along! – every step of the way by my Executive Assistant of twenty-six years, Anne O Broin.

My thanks must also go to my former Superquinn colleagues Keith Harford and James Burke, who worked side by side with me on the television series, and to my good friend and colleague Vincent O'Doherty who agreed to proofread this book for me. I am sincerely grateful to them for all of their insightful comments and suggestions along the way.

Knowing that I had access to all of the above resources really was a critical factor for me as I put this book together.

But there is one other group who deserve my thanks above all. They are the retailers, their families and teams who took part in my television series. Without their willingness to learn how to truly listen to their customers, and their genuine openness to new ideas, this would be a very different book indeed.

And for that I am eternally grateful.

NOTES

NOTES

NOTES

NOTES

NOTES

NOTES

NOTES

NOTES

NOTES

NOTES

NOTES

NOTES